Eleanor Louisa Lord

Industrial Experiments in the British Colonies of North America

Eleanor Louisa Lord

Industrial Experiments in the British Colonies of North America

ISBN/EAN: 9783337151492

Printed in Europe, USA, Canada, Australia, Japan

Cover: Foto ©Suzi / pixelio.de

More available books at **www.hansebooks.com**

INDUSTRIAL EXPERIMENTS

IN THE

British Colonies of North America.

BY

ELEANOR LOUISA LORD.

Bryn Mawr College, 1896.

—

BALTIMORE
THE JOHNS HOPKINS PRESS
1898

JOHNS HOPKINS UNIVERSITY STUDIES

IN

HISTORICAL AND POLITICAL SCIENCE

HERBERT B. ADAMS, Editor

History is past Politics and Politics are present History.-- Freeman

---

EXTRA VOLUME

XVII

CONTENTS.

PART II.

THE METHODS ADOPTED BY THE GOVERNMENT TO ENCOURAGE THE PRODUCTION OF NAVAL STORES.

CHAPTER I.— THE ENCOURAGEMENT OFFERED TO IMPORTERS IN THE FORM OF BOUNTIES AND EXEMPTION FROM DUTIES.

CHAPTER II.—THE PRESERVATION OF THE WOODS.

PART III.

THE CONFLICT OF COMMERCIAL INTERESTS BETWEEN THE COLONIES AND THE MOTHER COUNTRY.

CHAPTER I.—THE GROWTH OF THE LUMBER TRADE IN NEW ENGLAND.

CHAPTER II.—THE RISE OF MANUFACTURES.

PREFACE.

It is my purpose in this monograph to describe the attempts of the British government to force upon their colonies in North America a new industry, which, it was believed, would materially benefit England by supplying the navy with materials usually purchased at high rates from Norway, Sweden and Russia, and at the same time provide the Americans with commodities to exchange for British manufactures. The success of these experiments varied according as the given enterprise helped or hindered the industries already developed in the colonies.

Briefly stated, the theory in accordance with which the commercial affairs of the plantations were regulated is this: Colonies should be made as subservient and as useful as possible to the mother country. In view of this end it is advisable to encourage the colonists to develop their natural resources, and the merchants to import from the plantations those raw materials that are not produced in the mother-country. For such commodities, when purchased from foreign countries, are paid for in coin; while colonial products can be paid for in manufactures. Such a system of exchange between a government and its dependencies cannot fail to be mutually advantageous. It is above all important, however, that the balance of trade incline toward the mother-country; and that the colonists be forbidden to engage in manufactures or to export their raw materials to foreign ports.

If this policy had been followed consistently and without intermission, the results might have answered more nearly the expectations of its advocates; but neglect of the plantations, on the part of the government, and ignorance of the industrial conditions in America favored the economic independence of the colonists. The sudden efforts of the mother-country, between 1763 and 1774, to enforce restrictive legislation after years of laxity brought on the Revolution : her attempts to compel the plantations to furnish stores for the royal navy, afford a no less striking illustration of the failure of government policy to coincide with the best interests of the colonists. Had the eighteenth century economists read aright the lessons taught by these industrial experiments they might profitably have made the application to the question of taxation, and learned discretion.

The main sources of my information regarding the production of naval stores are the original documents known as the "Board of Trade Papers," now in the custody of the Public Record Office, London. For contemporary opinion upon colonial policy I have consulted the most noteworthy pamphlets and treatises relating to the colonies; and for a modern treatment of the subject I am especially indebted to Dr. Wm. Cunningham's "Growth of English Industry and Commerce."

I wish to acknowledge my obligation to Prof. H. B. Adams, of the Johns Hopkins University, for his courtesy during the preparation of this volume for the press; and to Prof. C. M. Andrews, of Bryn Mawr College, who has read both manuscript and proof, and assisted me at every point by criticism and advice.

ELEANOR L. LORD.

Baltimore, February 4, 1898.

PART I.

CHAPTER I.

FROM THE SETTLEMENT OF THE COLONIES TO THE END OF THE SEVENTEENTH CENTURY.

It is interesting to note that, as the romantic spirit which characterized the colonists of Raleigh's generation gave place to the more practical enterprise of the chartered trading companies which proposed to settle and exploit the new world called America, there was a corresponding change in the estimate of the relative importance of the new country's resources. While the accumulation of the precious metals continued to hold high rank in the economic creed of the day, the men who chiefly had to do with colonial enterprises no longer dreamed of increasing the treasure of the kingdom exclusively from the gold and silver and precious stones of the new world. The attention of the Lords Commissioners of Trade and Plantations and that of the planters themselves was directed, rather, to the development of the agricultural resources and the raw materials of the country. Of the natural products of the soil, the timber along the entire stretch of the Atlantic seaboard by reason of its abundance and variety was bound to challenge notice as suitable not only for building material, but for the equipment of the royal navy. We have only to read Hakluyt's "Voyages," to find that even in the sixteenth century the discoverers had an eye to the masting and caulking of Gloriana's ships, when they made their inventories of the products of Virginia.[1] During the period of actual settlement the importance of the trade in naval stores appears to have been plainly recognized. Although the New England charter of 1620 makes no mention of woods or timber, the charter of Massachusetts Bay, granted

[1] Hakluyt, "Voyages of the English Nation to America," Vol. II, pp. 301-327.

nine years later, specifies woods and wood-grounds among the appurtenances of the grant; while among the articles and "necessary persons" enumerated in the "Records of the Massachusetts Bay Company" to be brought over to the settlement, are mentioned "men skylfull in making of pitch."[1] By 1691, when the second charter was granted to Massachusetts, the importance of the "king's woods" had become so obvious that a special clause—destined by reason of its ambiguity to cause infinite mischief some twenty years later—provided for the strict reservation of timber for the royal navy.[2]

In 1633 Emanuel Downing, writing to Secretary John Coke with reference to the attempt of Gorges and Company to overthrow Winthrop's patent or to have another government established, observed that the whole trade of the plantations was maintained by undertakers in England who intended to persuade the planters to accept a new patent, and thereby be bound to transport no masts, etc., for cordage and shipping but to Old England; that the proprietors were desirous of royal protection against foreign enemies and of an extension of the patent a little to the north "where are the best firs and timber." "Let this corporation," he says, "but enjoy the liberty of their patent and to choose their own officers as every corporation does here. Then shall this kingdom clearly gain by the fruits of their labours that commodious trade of cordage, pitch and tar."[3] Two years after the date of this letter a ship brought the first masts from New England ; "and now," writes Mr. Downing again, "the trade being by us discovered, there is fear that the Dutch will use their wits to appropriate it." But if the plantation "prosperously proceeds," he doubts not but that England will make good that trade against Dutch and French.[4] Further testimony comes from one Thomas Morton, Gentleman, of

---

[1] Mass. Records, Vol. I, p. 24.
[2] Cf. Part III, ch. 1, page 109 *et seq.*
[3] Emanuel Downing to Secretary John Coke, Sainsbury, "Calendar of State Papers," Vol. 119, Sect. 119.
[4] Ibid.

Clifford's Inn, who, in 1632, wrote a discourse on the "New English Canaan," in which an entire chapter is devoted to a detailed description of the trees of New England. There are two sorts of oaks, he observes, excellent for ship or house building, besides ash for oars and staves; and there are pines in infinite store in some parts, of which may be made rosin, pitch and tar, "which are such useful commodities that if we had them not from other countries in amity with England our Navigation would decline. Then how great the commodity of it will be to our Nation to have it from our owne, let any man judge." Here is a very early appearance of the argument so emphatically urged by later writers in favor of importing naval stores from the American plantations instead of depending on the northern crowns for supplies. The writer notes that the spruces which abound in the north have been approved by workmen in England as more tough than those they have out of the East Country—"they are big enough to make masts for the biggest ship that sayles on the maine Ocean, without piecing, which is more than the East Country can afford; and seeing that navigation is the very sinneus of a flourishing Commonwealth, it is fitting to allow the spruce tree a principall place in the catalogue of commodities."[1]

By 1653, the government had begun to take a more active interest in the encouragement of American products. The Council of State in this year informed the Governors and Commissioners of the United Colonies of New England that they had taken into consideration "the need the Government has for tar, masts, deals, etc., and how they may remove all possible obstructions to the importation of the same from the plantations."[2] A ship was, at the same time, sent to New England for 10,000 barrels of tar and other commodities. An entry in the Colonial Records, dated November 17, 1653, shows an item of

---

[1] "Tracts and Other Papers Relating to the Colonies in North America." Vol. II, No. 5.

[2] The Council of State to the Governors and Commissioners of the United Colonies of New England, Calendar of State Papers, Vol. 119, Sect. 202.

money received for masts, tar, etc., shipped to England, amounting to £1,368 16s. 1d.; also, an invoice of serges, cloth, rugs, and blankets to be disposed of to procure masts.[1]

All the early accounts credit New Hampshire and parts of Maine with the finest timber for masts. Robert Mason in his "Account of New Hampshire," in 1671, says: "They export 200,000 tons of deal and pipe staves and ten ship-loads of masts yearly."[2] The infinite abundance and large size of the trees, together with the nearness of the forests to the Piscataqua, settled the question of the chief source of the mast supply in the American colonies, if the difficulties in the way of importing from so great a distance could be met, so as to make such an enterprise pay. There was good timber in New York,—in fact, a ship-load arrived in England from that province in 1675, and was pronounced at the navy yard at Deptford very good of its kind;[3] but the export from New York never compared with that from New Hampshire, owing, probably, to the difficulties of water-carriage.

Massachusetts yielded pine trees and other timber, to a certain extent, which were traded off to other colonies for sugar or tobacco; and there seems to have been a considerable quantity of tar and pitch made, but probably not for exportation. In 1672, it was enacted that the townsmen of Plymouth should be allowed to make annually ten barrels of tar, and no more."[4] No reason is given for this restriction, which, if not removed, must have fallen into abeyance, for in the "Notes on Plymouth," published by the Massachusetts Historical Society, the following memorandum is made against the date, 1687: "Tar, at this period, was made in quantities: notices of it frequently occur as being accepted in payment of salaries, 'as it shall be sold at Boston;' it continued to be made in less quantity, down to 1750."[5]

[1] Calendar, Vol. 119, Sect. 202, Annex II, III.
[2] Calendar. (1669-1674), Sect. 87.
[3] Calendar, Letter to Gov. Andros, Vol. 119, Sect. 669.
[4] Mass. Hist. Society Publications, "Notes on Plymouth," Second Series, Vol. III.
[5] Ibid.

But it was Carolina that excelled in the production of the pitch and tar, just as New Hampshire was the great source of masts and ship timber. The timber of the Carolinas was of no mean quality, and the soil was said to be admirably adapted to growing hemp and flax, so that these provinces were early looked upon as a possible source of supply for the royal navy By the beginning of the eighteenth century, pitch, tar and timber were counted among the chief products of Carolina. In Virginia and Maryland, naval stores competed with tobacco, but the latter was regarded as the more important staple. In 1664, when, in consequence of over-production, the price fell so low that the planters found themselves £50,000 in debt, a memorial on the subject was sent to the Lords Committee of Trade, at Whitehall; whereupon, after careful consideration, their Lordships saw fit to submit to His Majesty, among other proposals, "that, for the encouragement of the planters to apply themselves to the planting of other commodities which may be of more benefit than tobacco, His Majesty would be pleased to permit that all the hemp, pitch and tarr of the growth production or manufacture of Virginia and Maryland, for the space of five years from the date hereof, might be custom free."[1] This report having been read, His Majesty and the Lords of Council gave directions, "for the time being, to permit and suffer all the hemp, pitch and tar of the growth of the said plantations, that should be brought into the kingdom during the space of five years from date, to be freely imported and unladed without demanding or receiving any customs or imposition for the same." Great caution was urged to prevent frauds. This liberality is an anticipation of the methods of encouragement which became a settled policy from the reign of Queen Anne to the American Revolution.

After the Revolution of 1688, we find William and Mary signing contracts with one or two London merchants to supply the navy with small quantities of ship-timber. William Wallis

---

[1] Bruce, "Economic History of Virginia," Vol. 1, page 390.

received such a contract in 1691,[1] and in the same year John Taylor, who as early as 1665 had sent samples of plantation timber to the navy, contracted to furnish two or three shiploads of yards, masts and bowsprits, annually, for five years.[2] Three years later Taylor sent a memorial to the Lords Committee of Trade, in which he states that he has been at great expense and trouble to start ship-building and trade in naval stores in New England; he suggests that, to encourage his enterprises, his commodities and ships be made free of duty and tonnage, and that the duties on rosin, pitch and tar from other countries be doubled.[3]

In the meantime, a number of merchants petitioned for contracts to import stores from the plantations. The chief of these petitioners was Sir Matthew Dudley, who, with a large number of gentlemen and merchants, had, just at the time of the Revolution, undertaken to obtain an exclusive patent for working mines in New England; not meeting with much success, they had subsequently renewed their application for a charter, substituting naval stores for minerals, as the commodities of their proposed monopoly. The history of their attempt covers a long period of years; therefore, partly to avoid confusion, partly to use the case as an illustration of a particular phase of the movement to develop colonial resources, it will be treated in a subsequent chapter.[4] The other petitioners did not apply for charters, but sent in bids to the Committee of Trade for contracts to furnish certain quantities of stores to the navy.

The number of proposals received early in the year 1694 evidently suggested to the Committee the usefulness of a discussion with the merchants on the subject of plantation stores, for they granted a hearing to all the petitioners, at Whitehall, on

---

[1] Copy of Wallis's License; Board of Trade Papers, New England, Bundle F, Document 35.

[2] Report of Admiralty on Taylor's Memorial (C:7) mentions this contract of 1691. Board of Trade Papers, Plantations General, C: 16.

[3] Memorial to Lords Com. of Trade. B. T. Plants. Gen., C: 7.

[4] Cf. Part I, Ch. II.

the 15th of March in that year.[1] Some eleven gentlemen were
invited,[2] and these presented their proposals in detail, in order
that the Lords of Trade might compare prices and be in a
better position to judge what encouragement might properly
be given to importers, and whether it would be better to recommend the incorporation of a chartered company, as Sir Matthew Dudley suggested, or to rely upon private contracts, according to the custom of the Navy in purchasing stores from
foreign countries. The New England agents, Sir Henry
Ashurst and Stephen Evance, vigorously opposed the granting of a charter to Dudley, and stirred up Massachusetts to protest against such a monopoly.[3] They devised all sorts of delays, and finally contrived that no final action should be taken
until Massachusetts should have time to send over a formal
argument against the proposed charter.

In the meantime, as another means of baffling Dudley's design, Ashurst and Evance themselves submitted proposals to
furnish stores. They got leave to send over for specimens of
stores to be tested by the naval authorities and compared with
the foreign products used by the navy; but when, after eighteen months, a scant ship-load was deposited in the navy-yard,
the samples were found to be of so indifferent a quality that
Ashurst and Evance desisted from further efforts in that direc-
tion.[4] It was plain that a considerable outlay would need to be
made by somebody, whether by merchants, by corporations,
by the planters themselves, or by the government, before stores
of a suitable quality could be imported for the royal navy. John
Taylor, the contractor, reported that in the estimation of ship-
masters one gallon of Swedish tar was worth two of New England tar, and that he himself sent over pitch and tar for use in
his own ship-building in New England.[5] The plank from that

---

[1] Notification from Board of Trade of a hearing at Whitehall.
B. T. Plants. Gen., C: 15.
[2] The gentlemen were: Dudley, Ashurst, Evance, Bernon, Taylor,
Allen, Warren, Nicholson, Paggen, Heathcote and Slye.
[3] Memorandum, B. T. New Eng., Entry Bk. A., January 15, 1694.
[4] Attorney General's Report. B. T. New Eng., A: 2.
[5] Letter from Taylor to Board of Trade. B. T. Plants. Gen., C: 19.

province was not considered the best sort, being, generally, wormy and red-veined, although there was, doubtless, plenty of good timber to be had if it were properly selected. Taylor was, as he stated to the Lords of Trade, bred to the trade of importing naval stores and undoubtedly "had a better insight than the gentlemen who expected a charter." He had very little hope that it would be possible for the kingdom to rely entirely on the plantations for naval supplies. He spoke "as a merchant who guides his trade to the measure only of profit," and he pointed out, as a problem he could not solve, the difficulty of bringing bulky goods from a very remote country as cheaply as they could be brought from the kingdoms close at hand. The cheapness of the East Country stores was enhanced by the fact that the desired commodities were more plentiful in Sweden and Denmark than they would probably ever be in New England; while labor, in the former countries, was not worth one-sixth as much as it was in New England. Moreover, two or three voyages could be made to the Baltic, and four or five to Norway, for one to America—a fact which greatly increased the cost of importation. If it were His Majesty's desire to be supplied from the plantations in case of necessity, and with more regard to the quality than to the price of the stores, Taylor thought that this might be accomplished by setting up at some proper place in America, possibly in New Hampshire, the manufacture of pitch and tar after the Swedish method.[1]

In March, 1696, an important change was made in the administration of colonial affairs by the appointment of a permanent Board of Trade and Plantations in place of the special committees which had hitherto kept the government informed of the state of the colonies. Upon this board devolved the duty of making, from time to time, specific inquiries into the condition of the several provinces, their resources and articles of export and import; and of considering plans for their improvement, *i. e.*, plans for making them more useful to Great Britain

---

[1] Taylor to Board of Trade. B. T. Plants. Gen., C: 19.

and for promoting their commercial welfare by any means not injurious to the interests of the mother country.[1]

The desirability of freeing the kingdom from dependence on the northern crowns in the matter of naval supplies, was early brought to the attention of the newly organized board; and, in spite of the sceptical views of Mr. Taylor and the failure of Sir Henry Ashurst's specimens to pass muster, there began to pour into Whitehall continual assurances that there would be no difficulty in supplying the navy from the plantations, if proper encouragement should be given by the government.[2] It was urged that Ashurst's specimens might not have been fair samples of what New England could produce, and that it was quite probable that the fault lay in the ignorance of the people, rather than in the resources of the country. At all events, the Board of Trade decided that the experiment of encouraging the trade in masts and the manufacture of tar and pitch by suitable methods might be worth trying. Accordingly, with the approval of the Admiralty, they determined to send commissioners to New England to make exact inquiries about what might be expected from that country, and to put the people in the way of producing stores of the proper quality.[3]

Accordingly, the Admiralty drew up instructions for four commissioners, John Bridger, Benjamin Furzer, William Partridge and Robert Lamb, the last two having been recommended by Ashurst, on behalf of the colonies, to assist Bridger and Furzer.[4] The object of their voyage, as defined in the instructions, was to introduce trade with New England in whatever naval materials that province could produce fit for the use of the royal navy; also, "to broaden their experience and add to their qualifications in such matters." They were directed,

---

[1] Documents relating to the Colonial History of New York, Vol. III, Introduction, p. 15.

[2] Memorial from Jahleel Brenton, B. T. New Eng., A: 10, and Proposal of Ed. Randolph, Plants. Gen. A: 2. Considerations offered by Colonel Charles Lidget, dated August 28, 1696.

[3] Communication from Whitehall, B. T. New Eng., A: 12.

[4] Instructions for Commissioners, B .T. New Eng., A: 18.

first, to make themselves thoroughly familiar with the best methods of producing such commodities. They were next to proceed to New England; there to find out accurately, by personal observation and otherwise, the amount of materials to be had and to examine the quality by comparison with samples of the best of each sort, which they were to carry over with them. Explicit directions were given for the selection of timber for various uses, and they were directed to tell the inhabitants the fault which had been found with their tar and, since this was the greatest article of consumption, to see if it could not be improved. As soon as practicable, the commissioners must ship some specimens to England for examination, together with a report as to what quantity of each the country could produce. They were also required to make particular examination of the king's reservation, to send samples of what might be had out of those woods, and to investigate the facilities for water-carriage and shipping. A strict account of all purchases and expenses, and a journal of proceedings must be kept.

Bridger, Furzer and Jackson (who seems to have been substituted for Lamb as a member of the commission) left England towards the end of the year 1697, but the ship in which they sailed was, unfortunately, blown off the coast of New England to Barbadoes, where the commissioners were obliged to land. Here Furzer died, and Bridger was taken ill, so that he and Jackson did not arrive in New England till May, 1698. In November of that year, Partridge and Jackson wrote that as this was not the proper time to cut timber they had employed the summer in viewing the woods of Massachusetts Bay and New Hampshire, where they had found vast quantities of excellent white pine for masts. They had begun to experiment with tar after the Finnish method and had prepared one hundred and forty trees. They had persuaded New Hampshire to pass an act to encourage the planting of hemp, and they hoped to accomplish the same thing in Massachusetts.[1]

---

[1] Jackson to Board of Trade, B. T. New Eng., C: 20.

July 2nd, Mr. Bridger wrote to the Board of Trade that he was working single-handed, since Furzer was dead and Partridge, though very ready to give him a guard, was himself occupied with his duties as Governor of Piscataqua; while Jackson, contrary to instructions, had been at New York all the time and had not helped him at all, so that he was "forced to do all alone and ride up and down night and day."[1] This does not agree with Jackson's own account, quoted above, but the delinquent may have appeared on the scene after the date of Bridger's letter. Another letter from Bridger, written at Boston, November 6th, relates that in a progress from Cape Cod to Rhode Island, a distance of two hundred miles, he found very little good timber. He had also traveled forty miles to the place where hemp was grown, to encourage the people and instruct them in managing their land, which was not in itself rich enough to produce hemp.[2]

On the 9th of September, 1699, Governor Bellomont wrote a letter to the Board of Trade,[3] in which he enclosed an encouraging but vague report from Bridger. Some thousands of trees had been prepared for making tar after the most approved East Country methods, but the result could not be determined. The hemp experiment he thought likely to prove successful. Rosin had been tested and approved, and most of the timber was considered to be of good quality. He strongly recommended that, as a matter of economy, the king build transports in America. He complained of the waste of the woods and the neglect of Brenton, the surveyor of the woods.[4] Lord Bellomont expressed his opinion that the investigation was

---

[1] Letter from Sec. Vernon, enclosing letter from Bridger, B. T. New Eng., Entry Bk. B., September 25, 1698.
[2] Bridger to Board of Trade, B. T. New Eng., C: 27.
[3] Bellomont to Board of Trade, B. T. New Eng., F: 4.
[4] Report from Bridger enclosed in a letter from Gov. Bellomont, Sept. 9, 1699, B. T. New Eng., F: 19, 20. Brenton held the offices of collector of customs and surveyor of the woods in New England about 1695. The importance subsequently attached to the preservation of the woods will be discussed in Part II, Chap. I.

very expensive and its progress slow. At Piscataqua he had
talked with Mr. Partridge, who owned that pitch and tar could
not be made in any quantity there because of the scarcity and
dearness of labor—there being only about seven hundred families in the province, and the price of labor being at least three
shillings per day.

In view of Bridger's complaints of his fellow commissioners,
it is interesting to hear through Lord Bellomont the version of
Partridge and Jackson, who insisted that Bridger, without consulting them in the least, carried on private management, drawing money and ordering what work he pleased to have done.[1]
Lord Bellomont had taken upon himself, as governor, to question Bridger about his accounts,—an interference to which the
surveyor decidedly objected, saying that he was accountable to
the Navy Board and not to Lord Bellomont. But the latter,
either from zealous care for the government's interest or from
meddlesome curiosity, insisted upon knowing what Bridger
did with all the money he drew. Bridger refused to give him
a particular account of his expenditures, but he did show him a
scrap of paper on which was written the whole sum drawn,
amounting to £1,010 18s. £1,000 had been advanced to the
commissioners before they left England, and Bridger had
drawn £450 for the hire of ships to send home the specimens,
making in all £2,460 18s. already expended. Bellomont said
that the purveyors were reckoning on £250 apiece for a year's
salary. One of Partridge's ship-loads was valued at £300;
therefore, Bridger's ship of half the tonnage should be worth
about £150. Lord Bellomont did not accuse the commissioners of dishonesty, but he felt very strongly that, through bad
economy, "the king's design had become very chargeable:"
four people were drawing pay for what one might do alone.[2]

The commission acted with no sort of co-operation, and
Partridge and Jackson sent home a report of their doings in
New Hampshire entirely independent of Bridger's account,

---

[1]Letter from Bellomont to Board of Trade, B. T. New Eng., F: 4.
[2]Letter from Bellomont to Board of Trade, B. T. New Eng., F: 25.

much fuller and more systematic.[1] They maintained that they
had showed Bridger where to get specimens and that he had
gone ahead in his own way without consulting them, and had
rejected the advice of Mr. Partridge, who had been twenty
years conversant with the woods and knew how to get the
specimens much cheaper. Therefore, not caring to share the
blame for his extravagance, they had got specimens of their
own. They had thought it best, however, not to send two lots,
although they differed with Bridger about prices; but Bridger
having, by exhausting his credit, failed to obtain transports,
they had offered to supply him if they might be allowed to send
their specimens on their own account. In their report, Partridge and Jackson stated the quantity, quality and prices of
New England products, with a detailed description of the navigable rivers near which the timber grew. Among the recom-
mendations which they offered to the Board of Trade were the
building of transports in New England and the employment
of soldiers to work at naval stores. The latter suggestion had
already been made with reference to New York by Governor
Bellomont, who now claimed that the idea was his own and
that Jackson and Partridge were "plowing with his heifers."
The commissioners' plan was to erect forts in Maine and send
over soldiers to garrison these as a protection to the frontier
in time of war, and at other times to cut timber or make pitch
and tar. Maine was then desolate after the devastations of the
Indian war, and it was suggested that poor families be sent
over to settle and to work on stores.

When the specimens sent by the commissioners arrived, they
were examined by the officers at Deptford and Woolwich,
whose criticism with a comparative list of the prices of each
sort of specimen and of the corresponding commodities used at
the navy yard was enclosed by the Navy Board with their own
report. A few of the specimens were acknowledged to be very
good, but most of the timber was found to be inferior to that

---

[1] Report of Partridge and Jackson, dated at Portsmouth, Sept. 25.
1699, B. T New Eng., D: 30.

usually bought for the navy and the tar was of indifferent quality. The Navy Board, therefore, recommended that the commission be recalled, "to ease the king of that great and growing charge, it seeming to be far from answering the service expected from it."[1] A letter from Secretary Burchett to the Board of Trade, commenting upon Lord Bellomont's charges of extravagance against the commissioners, observes that "they have been sent for and their expenditures will be strictly inquired into."[2] In 1702, after having spent five years in New England, Mr. Bridger returned to England and presented his accounts.[3] Two years of altercation followed, because many of the disbursements had been recorded without the proper vouchers which the Navy Board required before they would confirm the accounts; but finally (1704) the Board of Trade recommended that Bridger be paid for the five years and three months of his actual service[4], at the rate of £250 a year.

With respect to one of the objects of their journey, the commissioners may be said to have been fairly successful. There was a prevailing ignorance in the mother country of the geography, resources and general condition of New England, especially of New Hampshire; and, although as a means of procuring information the commission was certainly expensive, its reports undoubtedly enabled the Lords of Trade to form a more intelligent opinion as to the possibility of depending upon the American plantations for naval stores.

---

[1] Reports from officers at Deptford and Woolwich, B. T. New Eng., F: 31.

[2] Secretary Burchett to Board of Trade, B. T. New Eng., F: 55.

[3] Minutes of Bridger's expenses, affidavits, etc., B. T. New Eng., N: 10, 19, 20, 26.

[4] Correspondence relating to Bridger's accounts, B. T. New Eng., N: 34, 35, 36, and Entry Bk. E., April 6, 1704.

CHAPTER II.

The Attempts to Form Chartered Companies for the Importation of Stores.

1. The Dudley Case.

The most noteworthy attempt to establish the trade in naval stores by means of a joint-stock company was that made by Sir Matthew Dudley and "some hundred notable gentlemen and merchants of London." The case covers a period of over seventeen years and admirably illustrates the attitude of the Board of Trade towards the proposal to develop colonial supplies, and their policy respecting joint-stock companies and monopolies. The gentlemen mentioned above, acting on information received from New England that some copper mines had been discovered in America, raised a joint-stock of £100,-000 and in March, 1687, petitioned for a charter to work the mines.[1] The original proposition had nothing to do with naval stores. The company evidently represented the substantial business interests of London and it included such men as Sir John Shorter, Lord Mayor of London, and Sir Humphrey Edwyn, Sheriff of the City of London.[2] A charter in thirty-three articles was drawn up, in which elaborate provision was made for the control of land, the appointment of officers, the power to make necessary regulations, and the erection of courts for dealing judicially with the concerns of the company and with crimes and misdemeanors (except capital offenses).[3]

The company desired that "all justices or other civil officers in any part of New England should be obliged to return any

[1] Petition of Sir Matthew Dudley and others for a charter, B. T. New Eng., Entry Bk. A., March 1687.
[2] Ibid.
[3] Copy of Proposals of the Petitioners, dated June 16, 1688, B. T. New Eng., Vol. 6, B: 23.

fugitives, workmen, or servants of the company; that sudden deaths should not be enquired into by the coroner of the place or colony, but by the coroner or other sworn officers belonging to the company; that deeds, fines and forfeitures appertaining to agents or servants of the company should accrue to the company exclusively; that they should have the right to try all civil pleas not exceeding £10, and not concerning title of land, which might arise between their servants and other inhabitants of the colony; that the workmen, agents and other officers of the company be exempted from serving on juries, inquests and sessions of any other than the company's courts: also from all ordinary military service by land or sea, except for necessary defense in case of invasion or open rebellion."[1]

The question which raised most doubt in the minds of the Lords of Trade, and of the Attorney General to whom they referred the matter, was how far such extensive powers would be compatible with the charters of the colonies in which such grants should be situated. Attorney General Powys reported his opinion that the powers specified would be too great for such a company in England, but not for an uninhabited country.[2] Accordingly, an Order in Council was issued to draw up a patent. This was done, but in the confusion of the Revolution, it was prevented from passing the Great Seal.[3]

On the accession of William and Mary, a second charter was drawn up for the incorporation of Sir Matthew Dudley and others under the name of the "Governor and Company of Adventurers for the Discovery and Working of Mines and Minerals in Our Territory of New England." The Board of Trade seem to have determined to favor the granting of this charter, and a warrant was made out for the king's signature, March 17, 1692; but "a caveat being entered at the Secretary's office by the Copper Miners' Company of England (on what ground

---

[1] Proposals of the Petitioners, B. T. New Eng., B: 23.
[2] Reports of Sir Thos. Powys, Aug. 4 and Oct. 2, 1688, B. T. New Eng., B: 23.
[3] Memorandum, Aug. 1688, B. T. New Eng., B: 1.

does not appear), the consideration of the differences between
them and the petitioners was referred to the Lord Chief Justice of the Common Pleas, and the Attorney General." Reports
from these quarters were so far favorable to Dudley's design
that Her Majesty in Council on July 7, 1692, ordered a warrant
to be prepared for the passing of letters patent.[1] But again the
petitioners were disappointed, for, as they affirm in a subsequent
protest to the Queen, another petition was presented, in the
petitioner's name and contrary to their knowledge, by some
"that were strangers to the former proceedings," which "begot
some difficulty in the dispatch of Her Majesties Gracious intention in favor of the Petitioners."[2] They therefore begged
for favorable action on their proposal, since it would be of great
service to Her Majesty's affairs "in a provision of copper, iron,
masts, pitch and tarr and other materials for Her Majesties
Royal Navy, as well as to the Kingdom in generall."[3] According to this statement, the scope of the undertaking had been
enlarged to include naval stores. The increased demand, due
to the French wars, and the continued petitions of other persons for contracts to furnish stores very probably account for
this addition. In May, 1693, heads of a charter were offered
by the Board of Trade to the Treasury for their consideration.[4]
The latter reported that it might be safer to defer the passing
of the grant until the government and council in New England
could be consulted. This caution was evidently the result of
the solicitations of Sir Henry Ashurst and Sir Stephen Evance,
agents for New England, who urged that the country be not
surprised by hasty action.

In January of the next year, the Board of Trade was directed
by the Council to set a time for hearing all proposals for bringing naval stores from the plantations, and to give fitting en-

[1] Memorial from Sir M. Dudley and others to Queen Anne, begging
for favorable action upon their petition, B. T. New Eng., Vol. VI, C: 5.
[2] B. T. New Eng., Vol. VI, C: 5.   [3] Ibid.
[4] B. T. New Eng., Entry Bk. A., May, 1693.

couragement to all who would undertake it.[1]   This seemed to be Dudley's opportunity, and his company now presented to the Board of Trade new proposals "for working copper mines and for making and producing all manner of naval stores in New England."[2]   In the meantime, Ashurst and Evance had offered proposals of their own, but they were put off by the Board of Trade with the excuse that it would be better to wait until they heard from the plantations.[3]   Dudley's new petition was handed over to the Admiralty, and in turn to the Navy, for inspection.   The petitioners also sent in to the Board of Trade a computation of the quantities of stores which they proposed to supply.[4]   Within twenty months after the charter was granted, they would undertake to furnish stores at the rate of 110 masts, 44 bowsprits and 75 yards the first year, and afterwards such quantities as should be desired, on twelve months' notice; also tar, pitch, rosin, and various timber of oak, pine and ash.   Nothing was said about copper or minerals, which seem to have dropped out of the scheme.   The petitioners begged for despatch.   The matter had been talked of for six years and the proposed delay until Massachusetts could be heard from was a mere idea of Ashurst to delay the charter.[5]   In May, Ashurst and Evance openly protested against the granting of Dudley's petition.

For the next two years, there seems to have been very little discussion of the subject of naval stores by the Board of Trade. In the spring of 1696, Ashurst's specimens from New England arrived at the navy-yard, but proved to be of little value.[6] At this juncture came the long expected communication from Massachusetts, expressing the views of the colony on the proposed Dudley charter, signed by William Phips for the Gov-

[1]Order in Council to Board of Trade to receive proposals for naval stores, B. T. New Eng., Entry Bk. A, Jan. 15, 1694. Cf. p. 6.
[2]Given in B. T. New Eng., A: 4.
[3]The history of their attempt has been related in Ch. I, p. 7.
[4]B. T. New Eng., A: 2.
[5]Dudley to the Board of Trade, B. T. Plants. Gen., C: 9.
[6]Cf. p. 7.

ernor and Council, and for the Assembly by the speaker, Nehemiah Jewell.[1] The memorialists said:

"Inasmuch as we have been informed by Sir Henry Ashurst[2] that the Attorney General, in his report, certified the inconsistencies of the petitioners' grant with the royal charter granted to the several provinces in New England; also how prejudicial the privileges and powers prayed for might be to their Majesties interests with respect to the government of that country, and other ways; and that the petitioners have waived and do not insist on most of their ten heads, yet pray to be incorporated with such capacities and liberties as is set forth in the said report, we shall only further offer to your Lordships, that all their Majesties subjects, singly or in company, have always had full liberty in trading, fishing, building ships, working, raising and gaining such commodities as they think meet; and their ships, when distressed, have been relieved, supplied, etc., and are under no restraint other than the Acts of Parliament for trade and navigation. We humbly conceive *** that it is requisite that the petitioners be, with respect of trade, in equal conditions and on the same level with other subjects; otherwise, with so great a stock as is proposed, the trade of the country will soon be engrossed and the commodities thereby advanced, to the utter ruin of the first planters, who, that they might free themselves from the yoke of arbitrary power then prevailing, and to augment the dominion of the crown of England, at their own cost transported themselves into this wilderness, subdued, planted, governed and with their lives and estate defended, and are still with their great impoverishment defending, against their Majesties cruell and treacherous enemies; *** and should the petitioners be incorporated, they can make no settlement to accomplish their ends, without acquiring to themselves considerable tracks of land. Many of the settlers have not been careful to secure titles to their lands. Now if the petitioners can make but a pretense of title, who will be so hardy, or can possibly be able to wage law and to cope with so opulent a corporation? Therefore, we humbly depend on their Majesties Grace and Favour that these plantations, already laboring under heavy persecutions, may not by such grants be discouraged and necessitated to conflict with the manifold inconveniences consequent thereof."

At the same time, Sir Henry Ashurst received instructions from Governor Phips to oppose the granting of the patent.

---

[1] The memorial is dated June 15, 1694. B. T. New Eng.. A: 7: New Eng., Entry Bk. A, fol. 14.

[2] Ashurst must have deliberately misrepresented the attorney's export.

This he proceeded to do in December, 1696, begging the Board of Trade, at least to delay the granting of the desired charter until the commissioners appointed to investigate the country should return.[1]

In the same month, the subscribers to the undertaking again petitioned the Board of Trade on behalf of their enterprise. They set forth the advantages of a joint-stock company, as against private undertakings, and agreed to have their charter declared null and void, if they could be proven to have wilfully broken its terms.[2]   In a memorial presented in April of the following year, by certain New England traders praying for military assistance for the colony, the opportunity was taken to protest against the Dudley charter as a "base monopoly of trade under the specious pretense of supplying His Majesty with naval stores, etc."[3]   On the other hand, Colonel Lidget, a New England merchant, in "Some Considerations for Advancing the Trade of New England," strongly advocated the production of stores by chartered companies,[4] and at the request of the Board of Trade, he drafted a charter suitable for such a purpose.[5]

The Board sent a draft to the Privy Council almost identical with that suggested by Lidget, with the addition of a number of clauses containing specifications for the employment of stock and for the quantities of stores to be imported within prescribed limits of time, together with several elaborate provisos to prevent stock-jobbing and frauds.[6]   A copy of these proposals was

---

[1] Protest from Ashurst against the Dudley petition, B. T. New Eng., A: 43.   See account of the commission, pp. 9–14.

[2] Dudley, etc., to the Board of Trade, B. T. New Eng., A: 47.

[3] Memorial from New England traders to Board of Trade, B. T. New Eng. B: 1.

[4] Considerations offered by Col. Chas. Lidget, merchant of New England, etc., B. T. New Eng., A: 34.

[5] Lidget's Heads for a charter, B. T. New Eng., A: 65.

[6] New Eng., Entry Bk. A, May 7, 1697.   The proviso against stock-jobbing ran as follows: " Provided always, and it is our will and pleasure that these presents are and shall be upon the terms and

offered to the solicitors of the patent, who responded with a memorial, purporting to represent "some hundreds of gentlemen, merchants, traders and others—subscribers toward the copper mines, etc." They set forth the advantages of a corporation over private individuals, and they answered the objections of the New Englanders that their trade would be interfered with, by affirming that, on the contrary, it would be increased. In the former trade, it was a few merchants that had raised the prices of English goods and driven the common people to attempt manufactures, because they could not afford to buy at such high prices. Moreover, some of the original promoters of the present scheme were men who might be supposed thoroughly to understand the interests of the country. Twenty-five years ago, the New Englanders had found it much to their advantage that an undertaking of this nature should be carried on. They had, in fact, by act of the Assembly given sole license and power of producing the same commodities to two or three merchants, excluding all others,—a much greater privilege than the present subscribers desired. Further, they could not learn that any of the many patents granted within the last few years had been clogged with such provisos, conditions and

---

conditions following, *i. e.*, that in case any members of the said Corporation, or Body Politique hereby constituted, or any person or persons whatsoever having or that shall have any part, share or interest in the Joint or Public Stock of the said Company (other than and except Executors and Administrators in right of their executorships or administratorships only) shall at any time or times within or during space of five years, to be computed from date of these presents, sell, alien, transfer, assign or any way depart with such, his, her or their share or interest in the said Joynt Stock or any part thereof unto any other member or members of the said Company, or to any other person or persons, bodies politique or corporate, that ther. in each and every case and as often as such alienations, assignments, etc., which shall happen within or during the said five years, all and every part share and interest of or in the said Joynt Stock so alienated, etc., shall from the time of such alienation *** become forfeited unto etc., etc." The king, if he chose, might under a specially recorded contract permit transfers after five years.

restrictions as it was proposed to insert in their patent. They thought that they had given the Board of Trade sufficient reasons to believe that the said undertaking was not "notional," and that stock-jobbing was not intended. They were willing to submit to reasonable restrictions and their later proposals fell far short of the privileges which the several favorable reports hitherto made on the matter had given them reason to believe it was intended to grant them. The inclination they apprehended their Lordships had to promote the undertaking, and the encouragement given had diverted them from applying to Parliament. They could not possibly accept a charter under such provisos as had lately been sent them, and if these were insisted upon they must wholly desist from giving their Lordships the trouble of any further application on that account. After so much time, trouble and expense, they would wait until they had an opportunity of representing elsewhere the great benefit which the said undertaking would prove to the king and all his dominion.[1]

The Board of Trade took pains to look up the case of monopoly referred to by the petitioners, and procured an attested copy of an act passed by the General Court of Massachusetts Bay, May 31, 1671, by which Mr. Richard Wharton and Mr. John Saffyn, merchants, and Company, were granted exclusive privileges to produce and sell pitch, rosin, oils of turpentine and mastick, for ten years, within the jurisdiction of the Court. The undertakers were granted the use of the pine or cedar trees within the compass of 5,000 acres of land, not otherwise granted, for their use in several places where they should find it most convenient, on condition that the commodities produced be sold at reasonable rates for the use of the country, and that they pay six pence per cent. of all the pitch and rosin made.[2]

On the 14th of September, 1697, the Board of Trade sent Dudley's proposals to Ashurst and Phips, for their opinion

[1] Memorial of subscribers to copper mines, etc., B. T, New Eng., B: 44.
[2] Copy of Act of Gen. Court of Mass. Bay, B. T. New Eng., Entry Bk. A, September 10, 1697.

whether such a charter would be in any way prejudicial to New England.[1] Ashurst acknowledged the receipt of the communication a few days later.[2] There was already in their Lordship's office an answer to those proposals, which, he says, "have been made to King Charles II., to James II., and to King William, but in each case, after mature debate in council, have been laid aside. If their Lordships have any new reasons for granting such a charter, they will receive answers from the traders about the city who negotiate with New England." He observes, in closing, that the commissioners are just ready to depart for New England. Ashurst wrote from Tunbridge Wells, where he was "drinking the waters," but he evidently hastened up to London to bestir the merchants to opposition, for, on October 2d, he sent the Board of Trade a detailed statement of objections, consented to by several inhabitants and merchants.[3] It was maintained that the patent was prejudicial to England and a ruin to New England, and that, by enhancing the price, it would obstruct the desired end of having naval stores from the plantations. Nine reasons were enumerated for withholding the charter:

1. "The gentlemen have taken over Sweads to work mines, but have been unable to separate the metal from the earth, and there has not been any copper yet perfected there. [4]

2. "The corporation do not propose to import above eight ship loads of stores for two years, which will not amount to above £6,000, which certainly may be within reach of two or three private merchants, without a corporation.

3. "The patent appears to be a monopoly, for it will lower the price of our nation's commodities, and the company's warehouse in New England will have all the trade, for they will think it to their advan-

---

[1] Wm. Popple, Secretary of Board, to Ashurst and Phips, B. T. New Eng., Entry Bk., A, September 14, 1697.

[2] Answer from Ashurst, B. T. New Eng., B: 47.

[3] Detailed statements drawn up by Ashurst and consented to by several inhabitants and merchants, B. T. New Eng., Entry Bk. A, October 2, 1697.

[4] This is the only intimation I have found of the company's making an actual beginning of their undertaking in America.

tage to sell cheaper than cost for two or three years, and so beat out every individual trader in New England.

4. "When they have engrossed the trade, they may set what price they please on English manufactures in New England, forcing the inhabitants to manufacture their own linen and wool to the great damage of England.

5. "In times of peace, the commissioners of the navy contract for not above two ship loads of masts in a year, which is of no great value.

6. "The people of New England are daily supplied by private hands with more commodities than the country can vend.

7. "None of these naval stores can be bought by a company so cheap as by private hands, on account of the great expense of such corporations.

8. "As to their promise to forfeit the charter in case of abuse of privileges, we have seen plenty of corporations misuse powers and survive twelve years of complaints to the King, Council and Parliament.

9. "The people of Massachusetts have already petitioned the king not to grant the charter, and even if these reasons have no weight, it seems unseasonable for the king to grant such a patent when he has just appointed a commission to go over and inspect the country."

As nothing more about the charter appears in the documents of the Board of Trade until August 6, 1702, it may be inferred that their Lordships acted upon the advice to shelve the question until the commissioners should have finished their work. In the summer of 1702, Dudley, encouraged by the fresh evidences of the possibilities of the country received from the commissioners, renewed his petition, reviewing the previous attempts "which, though approved in general, met with opposition from certain persons for private interests."[1] One cannot but wonder at the persistency of these gentlemen, in the face of such determined opposition. Eight of the original subscribers whose names appear in the petition of 1688 clung to the project; and the fact that these claimed to represent several hundred other merchants and gentlemen, on both sides of the water, is significant. There must have been a strong business faith that the scheme was workable and that, when effected, it would be profitable. Fifteen years of waiting had not quenched their zeal.

---

[1] Order in Council on Sir M. Dudley's petition, B. T. New Eng., L: 15.

The renewed petition was referred to the Board of Trade, who wrote to Mr. Wharton, the company's agent, requiring that a draft of such a charter as the petitioners desired be laid before them.[1] Mr. Wharton complied at once, and submitted a draft similar to those previously drawn up, but omitting certain provisions, which the Board required to be added before they would consider the charter. They insisted that the joint-stock should not exceed £20,000; that other persons or corporations be not excluded from trading; that adequate provision be made against stock-jobbing; and that specifications of the amounts to be sent home be stated.[2] Mr. Wharton sent a memorial to the Board, in which he remarked that the undertaking being to serve the kingdom, the petitioners had hoped that their Lordships would rather have encouraged them by the addition of privileges, than discouraged them by exacting obligations to perform particular matters within limited times and by restraining them from the general right of trade in disposing of their property as their necessities might require. But they agreed to certain specifications, viz., to prevent the mischief of stock-jobbing frauds by inserting a clause to the effect that all sales be entered in the company's book within six days after the contract was made, the seller and the buyer to take oath before the Governor, Deputy Governor or any two assistants when the contract had been made; and that all other contracts be null and void.[3]

The undertakers, as a body, also memorialized the Board of Trade.[4] They expressed their surprise that a design, admitted to be of public benefit to the nation and to the plantations, should meet with so much discouragement as the alterations and amendments made by their Lordships involved, which so effectually cramped and baffled the undertaking. They were

---

[1] Letter from Board to Mr. Wharton, agent of the Dudley company, B. T. New Eng., L: 16.

[2] Communications from Mr. Wharton to Board, B. T. New Eng., L: 17, 18.

[3] Mr. Wharton to the Board of Trade, B. T. New Eng., L: 19.

[4] Memorial from the petitioners, B. T. New Eng., L.: 22.

forced to conclude, either that their Lordships had not thought
the practicableness of it worthy of their consideration, or that
they had looked on the petitioners as wanting integrity or estate
to bring it to perfection. Taking up the alterations in order,
they commented upon them. If denied power to purchase
lands, goods and chattels, they could neither settle any facto-
ries, which were absolutely necessary, nor sow any hemp, nor
buy any naval stores; in regard to the refusal of waste lands,
mines and minerals, these were of no use to the crown and
would not be in many generations, but the company would
waive this point; thirdly, the restriction of stock to £20,000,
without farther increase, was inconsistent with the interest of
the Board, as well as that of the undertakers, for the specifications required the yearly importation of stores enough to
amount to above £30,000, prime cost, in the first two years, and
afterwards above £40,000. So small a stock would be eaten up
by the necessary charges and accidents; again, no clause like
that forbidding the transference of stock for five years had ever
yet appeared in any charter, and would crush the undertaking,
for it would mean an abridgment of the common right of subjects to transfer or dispose of property, which no man of abil-
ity would submit to; this would exclude many wealthy and desirable men. Lastly, they considered that the clause requiring
the vacation of the charter in case of misuse of power would
render the patent too precarious, and expose them to an incon-
veniency not foreseen by their Lordships, viz., the loss of stock
if the complaints of private individuals were allowed to prevail.
If these amendments were insisted upon, they must either desist from the undertaking, or make fresh application where they
hoped so advantageous a plan would meet with more encouragement. Mr. Wharton acquainted the Board, a few days
later, that they would agree not to exceed £100,000 stock without a special license from the crown. This amount had been
expressly specified in all the former applications, and no objections had ever been raised.[1]

---

[1] Wharton to the Board, B. T. New Eng., I.: 41.

Massachusetts was not to be caught napping, and William Phips promptly sent another protest against this charter, on the same grounds as before,[1] while at the same time a body of merchants requested the Board of Trade not to report favorably.[2] Phips maintained that the waste lands desired by the company had already been granted to Massachusetts. On the 8th of February, 1703, a further memorial was received from the subscribers, insisting on the necessity of £100,000 stock, and urging that their proposed restriction on stock-jobbing would be sufficient. To prove the first of these assertions, they enclosed an estimate of the probable cost of the undertaking for the first two years. The total amount was £171,400.[3]

The Board of Trade, after a careful consideration of both sides of the question, revised the charter, inserting such amendments as they saw fit, and submitted it to the Queen.[4] The arguments of the company had apparently prevailed, so far as to lead the Board to make certain concessions. The power of purchasing land in England or America was now allowed, to the value of £5,000 per annum; also, the transference of property. In regard to the joint-stock, the provisions were fairly liberal. The company were to be granted "full power and authority to raise a joint-stock in order to manage and carry on the affairs of the company from time to time for the ends and purposes for which the said company is erected; and the same joint-stock to augment and increase or reduce and diminish from time to time as they, the said governor and company, shall find most fitting and convenient,—the sum not at any time to exceed £100,000 to be underwritten here in England, and the further sum of £50,000 to be underwritten by any of our subjects in America for which purpose books are to be sent to Boston in

[1] Protest from Phips, B. T. New Eng., L.: 43.
[2] Protest from Merchants of Mass., B. T. New Eng., L.: 44.
[3] B. T. New Eng., L.: 49.
[4] Representation to the Queen from Board of Trade, enclosing draft of proposed charter, B. T. New Eng., Entry Bk. D, fols. 410–443.

New England, to lie open there for the space of six months. The present incorporation of the company shall not, however, be understood to be exclusive to any other persons from trading in the same commodities." The charter specified the amounts of each commodity to be brought to England within definite periods, and forbade exportation to any other country or place. The question of stock-jobbing was dealt with in a provision, that no person having any interest or share in the stock should at any time within five years sell or alienate any part of it on pain of forfeiture. A form was prescribed for sales or transfers at the expiration of the term of five years. The clause whereby abuse of the powers of the charter was punishable by forfeiture of the charter was retained, with a time limit of eighteen months.

On reading the Board of Trade's report and enclosures, the papers were referred, by an Order in Council, to the Attorney General and the Lord High Admiral, for their criticism.[1] The Lord High Admiral reported his opinion, that if the petitioners would contract to furnish certain quantities of tar, pitch and other stores as cheap as these were then purchased from the East Country, the Board might come to terms with them; but they must be obliged to furnish the largest masts, such as were supplied by Taylor and Wallis, and they must not raise the price.[2] The subscribers consented to submit to a clause obliging them to import masts of the largest size at current prices; also, to give Her Majesty a pre-emption, although they could not see why they should be obliged not to raise the price: they were much more likely to reduce it. In view of the retraction of the clause about restraining assignments for the first five years, they offered, as an expedient against frauds, a clause disabling all persons who should sell any part of their stock from directly or indirectly purchasing any stock within one year, under penalty of forfeiture ; and obliging any one to whom

[1] Royal order to the Board of Trade, B. T. New Eng., M: 2.
[2] Report of the Lord High Admiral, B. T. New Eng., M: 7.

stock should be transferred to take oath for whose use and benefit it was so transferred.[1]

While the negotiations for the Dudley charter were going on, the war of the Spanish Succession broke out, and the equipment of the navy became a matter of pressing importance.[2] As, at about the same time, several other proposals for importing American stores were submitted to the Board of Trade, which, on account of the dearness of Swedish tar, seemed well worth consideration,[3] the Queen commanded their Lordships to report their opinions whether pitch and tar might not be obtained from the American plantations and what were the best means for importing the same.[4] The Board therefore prepared a statement of their proceedings in the Dudley case, and their views on the subject of the importation of stores from America.[5] They said that they had brought the petitioners to agree to all the proposed restrictions except the stock-jobbing clause, which still remained undetermined. They were of the opinion that nothing could be more advantageous than bringing stores from America, thus preventing the exports of bullion to the East Country. Yet, inasmuch as that trade from the plantations was under great discouragement, by reason of the dearness of freight and labor, they did not see how the same could be set on foot with success, unless the public should bear some part of the charge (i. e., by premiums).

There is complete silence on the Dudley case in the Board of Trade records until the 18th of March, 1704, when the Board again laid before the Council a summary of their proceedings in the matter of naval stores.[6] In this report they reminded the

---

[1] Memorial from Subscribers to Board of Trade, B. T. New Eng., F: 8.

[2] Cf. p. 56 *et seq.*

[3] Proposals from Bridger, Haynes and others, B. T. New Eng., N: 2, 3, 4, 5, 9.

[4] Secretary Hedges to Board, B. T. New Eng., N: 1.

[5] Reply to Secretary Hedges's letter, B. T. New Eng., N: 4.

[6] Summary of proceedings on the Dudley case, B. T. New Eng., Entry Bk. E.

Council that they had last November submitted an account of the petition of Sir Matthew Dudley and others for a charter. Since then it had been proposed that, instead of the stock-jobbing clause, the petitioners should give personal security for importing the specified quantities of masts, pitch, tar, hemp, etc. This they had likewise declined, so that the Board had little reason to expect any success from those proposals.

I find no mention of the case after this date, except an allusion to the failure of the undertaking, in a letter written from New Hampshire and dated July 10, 1720, in which the writer, commenting on the encouragement of husbandry and the woolen manufacture in the several colonies, says that this would not have happened if the scheme of Matthew Dudley and Company had not fallen through by obstructions at home.[1]

2. The Pennsylvania Company.

There was only one other important attempt to form a chartered corporation to import American naval stores. This was the case of Thomas Byfield and Company, merchants, who were already trading with Pennsylvania, Carolina and the islands, on a joint stock of £20,000. Carolina has already been mentioned as the chief pitch and tar producing colony, and Byfield's design to extend the scope of the company's business by doubling their stock and developing a trade in those commodities, represents an effort to do in the south what Dudley's Company had hoped to do in New England. Whether Mr. Byfield was aware of the history and fate of the New England project and was sanguine enough to suppose that he could succeed where others had failed, it is impossible to say. He certainly made no attempt to obtain exclusive privileges, although he insisted upon the necessity of a charter, in consideration of the uncertainty and expense which must unavoidably attend the opening up of a practically new line of trade.[2] There were some favorable conditions which may have led him to

---

[1] Deputy Surveyor Armstrong to the Board, B. T. New Eng., X: 80.
[2] Memorial of Thomas Byfield, received Feb. 28, 170½, B. T. Proprieties, M: 16.

hope for success. The irritation of the British government at the Swedish monopoly of pitch, tar and other stores had rendered the desirability of obtaining such supplies from their own plantations more than usually apparent.[1] Applications for contracts to furnish stores were constantly being made to the Board of Trade, and it must have seemed to the Pennsylvania Company that there was an excellent opening for them. They were already well established in trade, and, therefore, had not to cope with some of the difficulties which a corporation freshly starting in business would have encountered. While they hoped to include, in time, the importation of masts, they applied for a charter authorizing them to deal in pitch and tar, commodities which were already reckoned among the chief products of Carolina.[2]

The proposals made by the Pennsylvania Company in 1703 offered the following terms to the government:[3] They would undertake to furnish 200 barrels of pitch at 18 shillings per barrel, and 400 barrels of tar at 8 shillings per barrel, delivered to the Queen's agents in Carolina, twelve months after notice could be given to their factors; or, if the government preferred to have the goods delivered in England, they would merely add to the price the usual freight and customs charges. They proposed to double the quantity the second year, and increase from year to year. They said that they had ordered sample masts to be sent by their factors, on information received that Carolina could furnish better masts than New England. If this proved to be the case, they proposed to contract for masts, as well as pitch and tar, at reasonable rates. In view of the "extraordinary charge of such an undertaking," they humbly desired a charter.

---

[1] Cf. p. 57 *et seq.*

[2] N. Carolina Records, Vol. I, p. 663. Lord Bellomont had called the attention of the Board of Trade to Carolina, intimating that he thought it might be best to get all the naval stores for the government from that province. B. T. New Eng., F: 93.

[3] Proposals of Thos. Byfield and Co., B. T. New Eng., N: 5.

This proposal was laid before the Board of Trade in November, 1703. In February of the following year, the company submitted in detail the reasons why they could not undertake to import naval stores without a charter.[1] In the first place, it was a great risk for a particular person or persons to make contracts with the government. Under their present constitution they had suffered for want of a charter, in having been forced to sell their goods in the name of private persons ; and they had sometimes found it difficult to get the money, they not being able to sue as a company for the same. Moreover, some were of the opinion that they were liable for the debts of one another, and that any member might be sued for what the company owed. They had managed with difficulty so far, but thought it would be dangerous to undertake greater matters without a charter; otherwise, they could not oblige the stock of the company to make good the contracts that might be made with the government. Further, a charter would give them the countenance and favour of officials abroad, and a better command over their factors. And finally, they expected to have to credit the government with large sums of money, which they could not pretend to do without a charter.

In March, 1704, the members of the company presented the draft of a charter such as they desired to the Board of Trade.[2] In general, the instrument resembles the usual form of trading charter, although, in some particulars, the Pennsylvania Company demanded rather less than Dudley's Company. Since they were already trading on a stock of £20,000, they asked for only £20,000 more to complete their stock. They did, however, desire authority to "assign and transfer the shares and interests of members in present and future stock, as well as to raise, call and pay money for an additional joint stock." They did not demand exclusive privileges, but they were willing to be obliged to import to the kingdom of England only; and they

---

[1] Memorial of Thos. Byfield, B. T. Proprieties, M: 16.
[2] Draft of proposed charter for the Penn. Co., B. T. Proprieties, M: 26.

would agree to give up their charter, if it could be proven at
the end of eighteen months that they had abused its privileges.
Enclosed with the draft was a form of obligation to the Queen,
by which five members (named) offered personal security of
£200 each, for the performance of their contract to import 1,800
barrels of pitch and tar, of the growth or product of Pennsylvania, Carolina, or other parts of America, before the 29th day
of September, 1706, "casualties of the seas, their enemies and
other inevitable accidents excepted."[1] Because a personal security was offered and exclusive privileges were not demanded,[2]
the Board of Trade were disposed to recommend these proposals to the Queen. Her Majesty referred the charter to the
Attorney General and the Solicitor General for their opinion in
point of law.[3] These authorities raised three queries which
they desired the company to answer: First, whether they were
willing to be obliged to import a fixed quantity of pitch and tar
annually, in all times of war, unless dispensed with by the
Queen. Second, whether they would agree to a proviso for dissolution on a notice, in case the Queen and Council should declare that the corporation was not useful to the importation of
naval stores. Third, whether they would oblige themselves to
deliver to the Crown a certain quantity at a fixed price, in time
of war, and a proportionable price, in time of peace, without
the Crown's being bound to accept it.[4]

The company felt that such close restrictions were unreason-
able. They did not care to undertake to import stores at all
times of war, unless the government would also be obliged to
take them at a reasonable price; for if they went to the expense
of setting up works in Carolina, and then the government should
buy of the Swedes, they would lose heavily. They offered to
import 600 barrels the first year and 1,200 the second, and then,

[1] Form of obligation to the Queen, B. T. Proprieties, M: 11.
[2] Royal order to the Board of Trade, B. T. Proprieties, M: 36.
[3] General report by Board of their action with regard to naval
stores, B. T. New Eng., Entry Bk. E, March 18, 1704.
[4] Queries from Attorney General and answers to the same, B.
T. Proprieties, M: 37.

after trial by the government, to make a new contract.   The
company were confident that they could lower the price of
Swedish Tar, and if ,after having done that service, they were
to be thrown over, it would seem very unjust; but they were
willing to be dissolved for misdemeanor or abuse of the charter.
They offered to give the government the refusal of all stores
which they imported, if the government would declare their ac-
ceptance or refusal of the same within a reasonable time.[1]

In December, the Commissioners of the Customs handed in
their report on the charter.[2]   In the first place, they observed
that some of the principal merchants had already withdrawn
from the enterprise. Moreover, certain other merchants had
sent in bids to furnish larger quantities at reasonable rates and
in less time, without a charter ; they were inclined to believe,
therefore, that this charter was designed for a private advantage rather than a public service of importing at lower rates.
They did not think it advisable that the petitioners should be
incorporated, when other very responsible merchants would
undertake the trade on easier terms for the government.   The
legal authorities made the further criticism that the charter did
not oblige the company to import pitch and tar for more than
the two years mentioned.   Moreover, there would be no point
in incorporating them unless they were obliged to import stores
during war, for in peace the freight would make the goods
dearer than those brought from Sweden. Certain other objections were raised relating to verbal ambiguities in the draft,
which the petitioners readily consented to alter; but on one or
two essential points they remained firm.   They would not admit
that their not being useful to Her Majesty was a sufficient reason for dissolution; for if they should succeed in forcing the
Swedes to lower their rates, the government would save a vast
sum yearly.   That, in itself, was no inconsiderable service; but
they were willing to pledge themselves to import a fixed quan-

[1]B. T. Proprieties, M: 37.
[2]Reports of Commissioner of Customs, Attorney and Solicitor
General, B. T. Proprieties, M: 50.

tity annually if they were not losers by the price obtained. They called the attention of the objectors to the fact that Swedish goods were paid for in money, while those from the plantations were paid for in the products and manufactures of England; so that the increase in the export of the latter commodities to the plantations would be enough to balance the bargain, even if the pitch and tar were not so cheap as the Swedish products.[1]

The subscribers showed a surprising indifference to the outcome of their petition, by observing, at the close of their answers, that although they could not effectually answer the interest of the government without being incorporated, they would desist from further prosecuting, if the granting were not convenient.

On the 14th of December, 1704, it was decided by the Queen's Most Excellent Majesty in Council, that the charter desired by Mr. Byfield and others was a matter for both Houses of Parliament, and therefore no order was given.[2] This action was a virtual admission that wider issues than the mere incorporation of a single company were involved: The question of naval stores was about to enter upon the parliamentary phase of its history,[3] which will be fully discussed in a subsequent chapter. In the meantime, without waiting for the final answer of the government, the Pennsylvania Company had, in the spring of 1704, gone so far as to purchase and fit out a ship to sail to Carolina for pitch and tar.[4] The ship was fifteen months making the voyage, because of waiting for the pitch and tar to be made, and a further delay of three months at Lisbon until a convoy could be found. On the arrival of the cargo, in July, 1705, the company petitioned the Board of Trade, that, inasmuch as their ship had brought in 400 barrels of pitch and tar before the pas-

---

[1] Reports of Commissioners of Customs, Attorney and Solicitor General, B. T. Proprieties, M: 90.
[2] Memorandum of decision of Council at St. James, B. T. Proprieties, M: 53.
[3] Cf. p. 63 *et seq.*
[4] Statement by Thos. Byfield & Co., B. T. Proprieties, N: 25.

sage of the Bounty Act, their case might be favorably recommended to the Commissioners of the Navy and an encouraging
price given. They had refused 50 shillings a barrel for it at
Lisbon, free of charge, in order that they might serve the government.[1] Whether their request met with favor does not appear; but they continued to trade in naval stores on their original basis, and five years later offered to contract with the
Navy. Mr. Byfield appeared before the Board of Trade in person, and "said in discourse that those commodities could not be
had in Sweden at the rates he offered them for."[2]

The history of the Dudley and Byfield petitions has been related with some detail, because the commercial problems which
they involved affected not only the importation of colonial products, but also the burning question of chartered companies; or,
in more general terms, the question of the best method of regulating trade in the interest of the mercantile system. So far as
the principles which underlie them are concerned, therefore,
the two cases may be treated as one. Matters were compli-
cated by the fact that several different bodies were concerned
with the final judgment of the case, and at least five points of
view were represented. The petitioners were, in the first in-
stance, brought before the Board of Trade; but that body could
only recommend to the Crown, *i. e.*, to the Privy Council, the
granting of such charters. The Privy Council made it a practice to refer cases requiring legal scrutiny to the appointed legal
advisers of the Crown. In this particular question of naval
stores, the Admiralty were immediately interested, and also, as
a matter of business, the Navy Board. When it is recollected
that just at the end of the century, Montague was making good
his affirmation that Parliament alone had the right to incorporate joint-stock companies, the complexity of the question
becomes still more apparent.

The Board of Trade, the Admiralty, the Navy, the Attorney
General and the Privy Council, who may be taken together to

---

[1] Memorial from Thos. Byfield & Co., B. T. Proprieties, N: 38.
[2] Record of attendance of Mr. Byfield at Whitehall with a memorial in behalf of the Penn. Co., B. T. Journal, N, p. 303.

represent the government, were the tribunal before which the case of the petitioners must be pleaded. The analysis of the argument on both sides would be somewhat as follows. The petitioners based their defense on the grounds of commercial expediency, supported by arguments to prove the advantages which the nation would reap from their success. The colonies, on the one hand, and the non-incorporated merchants on the other, appeared as witnesses against them. As business men, the petitioners without doubt put their own interest before that of the kingdom. They would not have ventured to float their capital, nor would they have argued their case so persistently, had they not definitely expected to make money out of the operation. The government rejected the suits of both Dudley and Byfield on the ground that they were seeking their personal advantage rather than the good of the nation. But it was hardly to be expected that any merchants, except, possibly, at a serious national crisis, would import merchandise at a loss, out of sheer patriotism. Self-interest was undoubtedly uppermost when the Dudley Company, perceiving that the working of copper mines was not a popular venture, seized upon the sudden interest of the country in bringing naval stores from America, and changed the character of their designs, in the hope that a naval store company would stand a better chance of obtaining a charter.[1] The first draft of their proposed charter implied the resting in the company of a power which was more than merely commercial, since it was to be based on extensive tenure of land. The New Englanders regarded the petition with great alarm, for the engrossment of land, disputes over titles, and the conflicts of the company with local authority which they foresaw, seriously threatened the interests of the colonies. Their protest was prompt and emphatic; and it was repeated at every opportunity until the danger was passed. The government tried to solve the land question by simply forbidding the company to purchase any land whatever; but Dudley remonstrated that such a restriction would make their undertaking quite impossible, and a limitation was proposed as a compromise.

---

[1] Cf. p. 17.

But there were other and more important grounds of opposition brought forward by the merchants, both in London and New England. The chief fear of the New England traders was that so large a corporation would monopolize trade and drive them out altogether. The company, they reasoned, would buy up English goods and sell them from their New England warehouse at less than cost, so as to ruin small traders. When this had been accomplished, they would be free to set whatever price they chose, which would end in forcing the inhabitants to manufacture their own linen and woolen,—a result as calamitous for England as for the colonies. The petitioners answered that, on the contrary, it was the few traders, who were then monopolizing trade, that set arbitrary prices. In the proposed scheme, the trade would be "dispersed into many hands." Moreover, the small traders who feared lest they should be crowded out were quite welcome to join the company. The government utterly refused to grant Dudley a monopoly, and Byfield never even asked for an exclusive charter.

During the first ten years of the Dudley case, the Board of Trade had, on the whole, favored the project in their reports; but they hesitated to give a decided answer. They wished to be perfectly sure that the accounts of the resources of New England had not been exaggerated; and Ashurst's specimens had not confirmed these reports. The Board sent over a commission to investigate the matter, and put off all the petitioners until the result of this inquiry should be known. The reports which came over were encouraging, and the specimens, though costly, on the whole met the approval of the ship-builders at Deptford.

The Navy preserved throughout a conservative attitude. They had no idea of serving the interest of any merchant or corporation; their business was to get the very best materials for the equipment of the royal navy in sufficient quantities and at the cheapest rates. They were responsible for the expenditure of public money, and it was a matter of indifference to them whether the stores came from Norway or New England, provided they were the best and the cheapest to be bought.

They always expressed a cordial sympathy with the policy of encouraging the importation of colonial stores, other things being equal; but they refused, as a board, to make any sacrifice of their business interests. This attitude the Navy maintained consistently throughout the period when the encouragement of colonial products took the form of bounty acts.[1] When the government became convinced that the resources of the plantations, if properly taken in hand, were really sufficient to supply the demand, they determined that the experiment was worth trying; but after they had finally committed themselves to the policy of encouraging the importation of stores from America, the doubt remained as to the best, *i. e.*, the cheapest, methods of attaining that end.

It must be borne in mind that the attempts of Dudley and Byfield to obtain charters were coincident with the struggle of the great Merchant Companies to retain their privileges. The Board of Trade and Plantations was organized at the time (1696) when Parliament was beginning to be suspicious of the dealings of these monopolists, and to question whether the commercial interests of the nation might not be better subserved if joint-stock companies were abolished and trade thrown open to all competitors.[2] The great monopolies had been sanctioned, originally, as the most proper mediums for regulating trade; but public opinion underwent a marked change toward the end of the seventeenth century, and so many charges of mismanagement and corruption were laid at the doors of the Merchant Companies, that Parliament interfered and began to assert that if trade were to be regulated at all, Parliament was the proper regulator. "A well ordered trade," says Dr. Cunningham, "meant an exclusive and confined trade ; open trade with all its faults meant expanding trade ; and Parliament, as representing the English public, decided in favor of expanding rather than exclusive trade."[3] The struggle of the

---

[1] Cf. p. 66.
[2] Cunningham, "Growth of English Industry and Commerce," Vol. II, p. 118 and passim.
[3] Cunningham, p. 38s.

East India Company for existence culminated in 1708, when it consolidated with the New Company which Parliament had erected in 1698. The combination, it is true, recovered exclusive privileges by an act of Parliament, but only in view of their important services to the government; and they paid heavily for their monopoly by assuming as their chief stock a large debt due from the government, on which the rate of interest steadily fell, so that the company found themselves trading on a dead capital.[1]

If such was the plight of the great Merchant Companies, smaller companies, like Dudley's or Byfield's, had little reason to expect exclusive charters. Still, the government was inclined to recognize the advantage of the joint-stock principle in undertakings which required large capital, and they incorporated several companies for the purpose of stimulating new industries.[2]

The Pennsylvania Company was in an anomalous position. It was really a mere voluntary association of merchants, who massed their capital in the joint-stock, but traded as if they were a chartered company. This does not appear to have been an unusual custom, and, although in a sense illegal, little notice seems to have been taken of the practice until it was forbidden by the Bubble Act (6 Geo. I, c. 18) passed in the interests of the South Sea Company, who complained of the fraudulent proceedings of these irresponsible companies. The government, when informed of the status of the Pennsylvania Company, inquired why, if they had traded so long without a charter, they could not continue on the same footing. Mr. Byfield's reply has been already quoted. It was, in substance, that for general purposes of trade, *i. e.*, exchange of merchandise, they had got on very well ; but they did not care to assume the risk of increasing their outlay in opening up trade in a new industry, without a charter behind them. If they undertook to guarantee that the products of their importation should be equal in quality

---

[1] J. E. Thorold Rogers, "Industrial and Commercial History of England," p. 124.

[2] Cunningham, p. 283.

to those of Swedish manufacture, there was much to be done by
way of improvement, and a further expenditure would be required for the regular production of these commodities on a
large scale, in view of a more or less constant demand for high-
class goods. The distinction between a joint-stock company
and a "co-partnery" was that in the latter each of the partners
was liable for the company's debts to the extent of his fortune ;
while in a joint-stock company each subscriber was liable only
to the extent of his venture.[1] It was chiefly on account of their
legal status that the Pennsylvania Company felt the need of a
charter of incorporation. But the government was not so much
interested in the merchants' point of view as in the making of a
good bargain for the nation ; hence, the fact that several private
contractors showed their willingness to make good offers without a charter militated against the petitioners for incorporation.
The Board of Trade was so determined to guard against the
evils of stock-jobbing that it would have effectually tied the
hands of the company with provisos and restrictions.

Inasmuch as the commercial policy of the day was not so
much to increase the nation's wealth by increasing the wealth of
individuals, as to establish national power by fostering national
resources, the government, consciously or unconsciously, settled the question by dropping the merchants and adopting the
bounty system, which, while it benefited the merchants as a
class, did not discriminate among them, but, as it were, distributed the inducement. By this action the government virtually
assumed the responsibility of developing the resources of the
American plantations.[2]

---

[1] Rogers, ch. VII.
[2] The methods which they chose will be described in Part II.

CHAPTER III.

Schemes for Employing Emigrant Labor in the Production of Stores.

Before entering upon a discussion of the policy which the government finally adopted, after consideration of the best methods for encouraging the production of naval supplies in the colonies, a little space ought to be given to an outline of two experiments which illustrate the application of the contract system to this undertaking. They represent an attempt to offset one of the chief obstacles in the way of manufacturing plantation stores as cheaply as they could be bought from the East Country, namely, the scarcity and dearness of labor. It was conceived that this might be done by transporting poor but industrious emigrants to some of the timber lands not already occupied, and granting them land on easy terms. The rent might be paid in the naval stores which the settlers were expected to produce after they had cleared land enough for their habitation and subsistence. It cannot be said that these projects were consciously fostered by the government to take the place of the proposals of the rejected joint-stock companies, but as they happen to follow the failure of these attempts, the natural chronological order will be observed.

The first settlement scheme was that undertaken by Colonel Hunter, who was made governor of New York in 1710. Before he went to New York, he submitted to the Board of Trade an elaborate proposition for transporting, at the expense of the government, 3,000 refugees from the German Palatinate to crown lands in New York, and employing them in the production of naval stores. The advantages of the scheme were many. In the first place, the Palatines would be provided for in such a way that the Queen's charity would be amply repaid, in time, by important services to the nation. The introduction of 3,000 persons would add materially to the strength and security of the frontier, and the cost of transportation and temporary maintenance would be more than met by the masts, tar, pitch and hemp in which the Palatines were to pay for their grants. The returns would necessarily be delayed for several years, but it was urged that capital so expended would ultimately be repaid with interest.[1]

The details of Colonel Hunter's plan were worked out as follows :[2] After the Palatines had been transported, they would be settled on such lands as were deemed suitable for their proposed occupation, and encouraged to work in partnership, i. e., five or more families in common. Forty acres per head would be granted to each family, under the seal of the province, for which the usual quit-rent would be expected, payable seven years after the date of the grant. The only condition of the grant should be the prohibition of any "woolen or such like manufactures."[3] Inasmuch as the people were wretchedly poor, it would be necessary to maintain them for a year or two at the public expense, because, until they should have built themselves huts and cleared land enough for tillage, they could not make much progress with the naval stores. The rate of subsistence suggested was six pence sterling per head a day, for men and women, and four pence for children. Colonel Hunter's estimate of the quantities of stores which the Palatines, when once established, would be able to produce in a year shows an optimistic faith in the success of the venture. He computed that one man alone could make six tons of stores in a year : a number of men assisting one another could double the quantity in proportion, so that, supposing six hundred men to be employed, the result of their labors would equal seven thousand tons a

[1] Address to the Queen from the Board of Trade, B. T. New York, Aa: 122.
[2] Ibid.
[3] It was observed at the time that the exports from New York greatly exceeded the importation of British manufactures.

year. In case more was produced than would be necessary for consumption in Her Majesty's dominions, a beneficial trade with Spain and Portugal could be maintained from the surplus. The commissioners to New England had reported that tar might be had under £5 a ton ; then supposing the freight in time of peace to be £4 a ton, which would be exactly covered by the premium recently granted,[1] there would appear to be no reason why tar should not be imported as cheaply as from the northern countries. The good quality of New England tar had been acknowledged, for, in the year 1707, 4,704 barrels were certified to be satisfactory enough to receive the bounty.

To bring the productions of the Palatines to perfection a considerable outlay would be necessary, at first, for the necessary supervision of the workmen and the disposal of the supplies when manufactured. As the people would have no knowledge of the proper methods of work, three or four skilled superintendents must accompany them ; or Mr. Bridger, the surveyor, might for a consideration come to the settlements with one or two assistants and teach the people how to go to work. In any case, it would be necessary to have a resident overseer to keep the people busy, at a salary of, perhaps, £100 a year. A temporary storehouse for finished productions would be needed at the settlement, and another at New York, from which the stores could be shipped. A commissary would be required at the latter place (at a salary of £200 for himself and clerk) to keep an exact account of the amounts received and the names of those from whom the stores were received and of those to whom they were delivered. The " neat produce of the stores," after all expenses had been paid, was to be handed over to the commissary, or other person appointed to receive the same, " to and for the proper use and behalf of such Palatines respectively to whom it doth of right belong." The Board of Trade was pleased to recommend these proposals to the Queen and Council, with the result that Hunter secured from Parliament an appropriation of

---

[1] 3 and 4 Anne c. 9. Cf. Part II, Ch. I.

£10,000 and entered into a contract to put the project into operation.[1]

When Colonel Hunter arrived in New York with his Palatines, in the summer of 1710, he found it no easy task to carry out his plans. The first difficulty was to find lands suitable for the agricultural needs of the settlers near enough to the pine lands, which, in turn, must be contiguous to navigable rivers.[2] The lands at the disposal of the Crown offered no such combination of advantages, and Hunter was forced to purchase 6,000 acres of the Manor of Livingston on the Hudson, for which he paid £400 (£266 English money).[3] Here he settled the majority of the Palatines in three villages, and the rest in two villages on the west side of the river. Mr. Bridger, who came to New York to assist Colonel Hunter, selected the first site and approved the other.[4]

Robert Livingston, the proprietor of the Manor, perceived an excellent opportunity for making money out of the settlement on his estate. There being a flour-mill and a brew-house connected with the Manor, he induced Colonel Hunter to give him the contract to "victual" the Palatines ; that is, he engaged to furnish each person, daily, with one-third of a loaf of bread (4½ pence size) and one quart of "ship's beer."[5] The settlers were provided with meat also, but I do not understand that Livingston arranged to furnish anything but bread and beer.[6] On the 14th of November, 1710, Governor Hunter wrote to the Board of Trade that the settlers had already built comfortable huts and were clearing the land, so that by spring he hoped to

---

[1] 8 Anne c. 14, Sect. 35. Roberts, "New York," Vol. II, p. 235.
[2] Doct. Hist. of New York, compiled by E. B. O'Callaghan, Vol. III, p. 651.
[3] Doct. Hist. of New York, Vol. III, p. 644.
[4] Letter from Bridger, B. T. Letters, November 10, 1710. Doct. Hist. of New York, Vol. III, p. 560.
[5] Doct. Hist. of New York, Vol. III, p. 653.
[6] The following account of the subsistence of the Palatines from

set them to work on the stores according to Mr. Bridger's directions.[1]

But instead of applying themselves industriously to producing stores for the royal navy, in gratitude for the asylum and subsistence so generously afforded by the Queen, the Palatines, contrary to the sanguine expectations of Governor Hunter, began to show signs of restlessness and discontent. Along with rumors of the expected conquest of Canada, they heard reports of broad, rich lands on the frontier and in Nova Scotia, which they persisted in believing to be the land referred to in the contract which had been read to them in High Dutch before they left England. They grew to regard their present location as merely temporary, and continually spoke of the "land of Canaan" to which they looked forward. Such an attitude of mind was fatal to any design for the regular production of supplies for the navy. Mr. Cast, who seems to have been the chief superintendent, overheard a conversation of some of the Palatines which revealed a point of view quite different from that of the promoters of the undertaking. The present site, they said, was well enough chosen for present purposes, but it was a

---

October, 1710, to March 25, 1711, as given in Doct. Hist. of New York, Vol. III, p. 657.

Year and Month.	Date.	No. of Persons Subsisted.	No. of Days.	At 6d Per Diem.
1710				£ s. d.
October........	6	213	26	138 9 .
"	9	111	23	63 16 6
"	12	118	20	59 .. .
"	14	72	18	32 8 .
"	16	50	16	20 .. .
"	25	703	7	123 .. 6
"	27	999	5	12 7 6
November.....	1	1,484	30	1,113 .. .
December......	....	1,455	31	1,127 12 6
1711				
January........	....	1,434	31	1,111 7 .
February......	....	1,435	28	1,004 10 .
March	....	1,437	25	898 2 6
				Summa, £5,703 13 6

[1] Doct. Hist. of New York, Vol. III, p. 654.

limited tract, and, while they were willing to remain there for
a year or two, they had come over to establish their families and
secure lands for their descendants, and they did not propose to
spend all their days on this spot making tar for the English
navy.[1] Those in charge of the other settlements found a similar
reluctance on the part of their laborers to "listen to tar-mak-
ing."[2] The system of enforced labor under constant oversight
was irritating, and Mr. Cast was particularly obnoxious to
the people. They began to complain, probably with reason,
that they were badly fed, and that they were not making any
money, as their contract had led them to believe they would be
able to do.[3]

The general discontent was fomented by one or two ring-
leaders, who at length carried matters so far that Colonel
Hunter was hastily summoned to quell a mutiny. Finding that
argument was a waste of breath, he had the contract which they
had all signed re-read, and he asked them to say decisively
whether or not they intended to abide by it, that he might act
accordingly. After some deliberation, they returned answer
that they were willing to keep their contract, "and so," wrote
Colonel Hunter, "we all parted good friends."[4] The peace was
not of long duration, and a fresh outbreak, three weeks later,
brought Colonel Hunter to the spot with a force of soldiers.
He disarmed the Palatines, but listened to their complaints.
They now insisted that they had been cheated in the contract,
which was not the one that had been read to them in England
and which would force them to remain on these lands forever.
They further complained that they had not received the promised food, clothes and tools, and that their people were dying
for want of care and remedies.[5] Colonel Hunter attributed
their discontent to their having been misled and frightened,
and he quoted facts to prove that their pretended injuries were

[1] Doct. Hist. of New York, Vol. III, p. 658.
[2] Ibid.
[3] Doct. Hist. of New York, Vol. III, p. 661.
[4] Doct. Hist. of New York, Vol. III, p. 660.
[5] Doct. Hist. of New York, Vol. III, pp. 660-66.

without foundation. The deaths and sickness had resulted from
a distemper caught on the passage over, for which doctors and
medicine had been provided. Mr. Clarke, Secretary of the
Council of New York, wrote an account of the mutiny to the
Board of Trade and expressed his opinion that the deprivation
of their arms would bring the Palatines to reason ; and, in a
second letter, he was able to inform their Lordships that the
more sober-minded had met together and resolved to beg the
governor's pardon. The governor forgave them, with the
understanding that the first disobedience would be punished
with the utmost rigor of the law. Whereupon the penitents
" began to demonstrate their sincerity by inquiring when they
should be set to work."[1]

For the better management of the Palatines, Governor
Hunter now formed a court, of which Robert Livingston was
to be a permanent member, to take cognizance of all misdemeanors of the people and for general regulation of their labor.[2]
The commissioners soon found matters to occupy their attention, such as the difficulty in getting the coopers to make staves
enough for the tar barrels. This they managed by detaching
certain men to work alternate weeks, requiring the list masters
to keep a strict account of each man's time. In July, 1711, Mr.
Cast wrote to Governor Hunter that the people were more sub-
missive, but that better meat must be provided. It was undoubtedly easier to retrench bad than good food, but matters had been
carried too far, and he begged that the people be relieved from
salted provisions. A bridge was being built to carry the tar to
the other side of the river. The people viewed this bridge with
suspicion, as an indication that a very extensive manufacture
of tar was contemplated, and they cynically remarked that it
would rot before it was put to that use.[3]

To make the affairs at the settlements worse, unfortunate
dissensions arose in the court itself. Everybody suspected his
fellow commissioners, while the cupidity and arbitrary behavior

[1]Doct. Hist. of New York, Vol. III, p. 667.
[2]Doct. Hist. of New York, Vol. III, p. 669.
[3]Doct. Hist. of New York, Vol. III, p 672.

of Livingston became daily more unbearable.[1] He had the reputation of being unscrupulous, and at the very beginning of the settlement Lord Clarendon had written to a member of the Board of Trade that he thought it most unfortunate that Colonel Hunter had fallen into the hands of such a man ; he felt certain that Livingston had contrived to offer the sale of his lands for the sole purpose of getting the contract to feed the Palatines.[2] Hunter himself now declared that Livingston had betrayed his confidence and misrepresented his character.

Discouragements multiplied. The winter of 1712 was a hard one ; the ice in the river carried away part of the corn-mill and the foot-bridge, and nearly broke the dam, so that it was difficult to get enough flour to feed the people.[3] By July of that year, it became necessary to retrench on beer and bread, and Colonel Hunter sent word to Livingston to give the dole only to the men who were actually at work, and not to their families.[4] The situation grew rapidly worse, and in September Colonel Hunter wrote to Mr. Cast that he had at last exhausted all his money and credit for the support of the Palatines, and had embarrassed himself with difficulties he knew not how to surmount, unless his bills of exchange were paid. But, trusting that the Queen would reimburse him, he was disposed to make some sort of shift, now that the work had progressed thus far. He suggested, as an expedient, that those who could support their families by hiring themselves out to farmers in New York or New Jersey, should be given a ticket of leave, with the understanding that it was merely a temporary arrangement and that there was not the least intention to abandon the tar works. The coopers and as many as it would be necessary to employ under them were to be retained. Hunter expressed his confident expectation that he could get his bills of exchange paid by spring, and be enabled to support all the Palatines. He

---

[1] Doct. Hist. of New York, Vol. III, pp. 673, 674.
[2] Doct. Hist. of New York, Vol. III, p. 656.
[3] Doct. Hist. of New York, Vol. III, pp. 679 to 681.
[4] Doct. Hist. of New York, Vol. III, p. 680.

said he had a good conscience that he had done everything he could to forward the undertaking.[1]

The Palatines were in great distress and considered themselves cast off by the governor.[2] According to their statement of grievances presented to the Board of Trade in 1722,[3] they were put under the hard necessity of applying to the Indians to settle on the tract of land called Schoharie. Permission was readily granted, and in two weeks all hands fell to work and, with great toil and almost no food, cleared a way fifteen miles through the woods. Fifty families went to Schoharie and were almost settled when they received orders from the governor that whoever went on that land would be declared a rebel. But, having made up their minds that to go elsewhere meant starvation, they continued operations ; and in March the rest of the people traveled through three feet of snow to join their friends in the "promised land." Their troubles had not ended, however, for they had to live for some time on the charity of the Indians. Then came claimants of the land from Albany, who, not being able to dislodge the settlers, tried to sow enmity between them and the Indians.

With the subsequent experiences of the Palatines we are not concerned here. Some of them went to Pennsylvania, where they were kindly received by the Quakers.[4] Those who remained in the settlement on the Mohawk as independent laborers became industrious and useful citizens.[5] The naval store project had ended in miserable failure, for reasons which the narration of its history readily suggests. There had been, practically, no return for the outlay of money, and Governor Hunter was over £20,000 out of pocket—a debt which he mentions in

[1]Doct. Hist. of New York, Vol. III, pp. 683-684.
[2]Friedrich Kapp, "Die Deutsche im Staate New York," p. 44.
[3]Doct. Hist. of New York, Vol. III, pp. 707-714.
[4]Peter Kahm's "Travels in America," quoted in Appendix X of Rupp's "Collection of Thirty Thousand Names of German and other Immigrants in Pennsylvania, from 1727-1776." Phila. 1876. Macpherson, "Annals of Commerce," Vol. III, p. 6.
[5]Roberts, "New York," Vol. I, p. 237.

his will as having been acknowledged by Mr. Harley and the Treasury, but never paid.[1]

The contract system had proved a feeble substitute for independent labor, for the Palatines were not slaves to be driven to work by overseers. And yet they were placed in the position of serfs, in that they had fettered themselves to the land by a contract which rated their holdings in terms of labor.[2]   It was originally intended that, after the settlements had begun to flourish and the manufacture of stores had begun to yield a profit above the debts and expenses of the Palatines, the surplus should be distributed among them as a sort of dividend.[3] But as that state of affairs never came to pass, there was little to encourage any enthusiasm for the work which they had been forced to undertake against their will.

Conditions not more favorable, perhaps, but different in character, affected the settlement of the lands between the Kennebec and St. Croix Rivers—a project in the interests of the production of naval stores which was suggested about the year 1713, when some disbanded officers and soldiers petitioned the government for a grant of land.[4] It was represented that the land near the mouth of the Kennebec was excellent, abounding in fine timber for ship-building and masts for the royal navy, while the soil was deep and suitable for hemp. Thomas Coram, the philanthropist, who as a merchant had spent some time in Taunton, Mass., interested himself in the scheme and with several other gentlemen renewed the petition on behalf of the soldiers, in February, 1715.[5] He proposed to build a royal town, to be called Augusta, with dwellings for five hundred small families. The total cost of the undertaking was estimated at £60,000. The wood which would be destroyed in clearing the

---

[1] Dictionary of National Biography, Vol. XXVIII.
[2] Kapp. "Die Deutsche im Staate New York," p. 108.
[3] Cf. p. 44.
[4] Petition of disbanded soldiers to Board of Trade, B. T. New Eng., T: 50.
[5] Proposals offered by Thomas Coram, B. T. New Eng., Entry Bk. H, February 10, 1715.

land would produce pitch and tar, and afterward such lands as could be spared from corn and pasturage might be tilled and sown for hemp, to pay rent to the king for the land taken up. No definite action was taken on this proposal, but the request was renewed in a more definite form, in 1724.[1] Each of the petitioners proposed to take over ten families of at least three persons. The cost of transportation was to be defrayed by the government, which would also furnish forts, garrisons, arms and ammunition ; and the lands were to be granted gratuitously, with merely a quit-rent of twenty-eight pounds of good hemp, annually, for every acre of land cultivated, this rent to commence seven years after the land should be cleared and made fit to bear hemp. They proposed to raise a fund to buy tools, fishing tackle and provisions, while the charge of transporting and maintaining the people was to be repaid in naval stores, after seven years.

I have been unable to find any satisfactory records of the history of this petition. Although approved by the Board of Trade, the project is said to have fallen through, owing to the opposition of Jeremiah Dummer, the agent for Massachusetts, who objected to certain restrictions upon the fishery.[2] There the matter rested, until renewed, in still another form, by David Dunbar on his appointment as Governor of the territory of Sagadahock (Kennebec), in 1729. The reason of this appointment was the determination of the Board of Trade to re-establish the fort at Pemaquid, which was considered to be an important outpost on the frontier. The old fort had been destroyed by the Indians forty years before, and ever since that time the Board of Trade had been trying to induce Massachusetts to rebuild it ; but successive governors had argued in vain. The Assembly refused to incur such an expense for a fortification which they held to be too remote for efficient protection. Failing to coerce Massachusetts, the British government decided to take the

---

[1] Answers by petitioners to questions put to them by the Board of Trade, B. T. New Eng., Y: 23.
[2] Palfrey, " History of New England," Vol. IV, p. 567.

matter into its own hands. Accordingly, Colonel Dunbar entered upon his task, and named the new fort "Fredericksburg."[1] Shortly after his arrival, a number of English and Irish families, some of whom had just come over, others of whom had been long settled in the neighborhood, on hearing of the erection of a new province under Colonel Dunbar's government, applied to him for grants of land.[2] He offered lots of from 50 to 100 acres per head, to each family, on payment of one penny per acre quit-rent to the king after ten years, subject to another penny, on demand of the king, for expenses of government. Dunbar was an energetic worker, and, having laid out three townships—Townsend (Boothbay), Harrington (Bristol), and Walpole (Nobleboro),—soon had 150 families settled.[3] He had been made surveyor of the woods in 1728, and was interested in the production of naval stores. After having ordered several acres to be prepared for hemp, he wrote home enthusiastic assurances that he should soon be able to send over good samples of hemp ; and he informed the Board of Trade of the abundance of timber, especially of large white pines, in the new province.[4] Owing to the fact that there had been no surveyor there to look after the woods, many of the finest mast trees had been wantonly destroyed to make shingles or canoes. There were said to be fine forests on the east side of the Kennebec which would be sufficient to supply the royal navy forever, if cared for ; and Dunbar suggested to the Board of Trade, that 10,000 acres of the best tracts near navigable rivers should be set apart in the new province as a nursery for the royal navy, until the resources of Maine and New Hampshire should be exhausted.

The Board of Trade adopted this suggestion and wrote back to Dunbar to lose no time in setting apart 300,000 acres, since

---

[1] Johnston, "History of the Towns Bristol and Bremen, including the settlement at Pemaquid."
[2] Colonel Dunbar was an Irishman.
[3] Paper by William Willis on "Scotch-Irish Immigration to Maine." Collections of Maine Hist. Soc., Vol. VI.
[4] B. T. New Eng., Z: 91. David Dunbar to the Board of Trade, America and West Indies, No. 1: 166.

the work was exceedingly important.[1] The progress of Colonel Dunbar's operations was unfortunately retarded by his quarrel with Governor Belcher[2] and by the disputes with the Massachusetts proprietors who claimed title to the lands about the Kennebec. Moreover, though vigorous and able in his administration, Dunbar had no tact, and he contrived to make himself very unpopular in Massachusetts in the exercise of his duties as surveyor of the woods. He believed, too, that the Massachusetts proprietors regarded his government of the new province as an usurpation and looked to Governor Belcher as the champion of their rights.[3] The latter had begun his administration by issuing a proclamation reminding the inhabitants of the land about Pemaquid of their allegiance to the province. The nature of the quarrel over the title to the Kennebec lands is not important in this connection ; but the hard feeling so increased, that in September of 1730 Dunbar wrote from Boston to the Board of Trade, that the disputes between the pretended proprietors and the new settlers was like to end in a kind of war. The former openly said that they would part with their heart's blood before they would give the king one farthing quit rent. Dunbar was informed by the advocate whom he consulted that if he should attempt to go to Fredericksfort, the Governor and Council would send a force to take it from him and make him prisoner. In view of this possibility, Dunbar applied for military protection to Colonel Philips, Governor of Nova Scotia.[4] Governor Belcher at once wrote to the Board of Trade utterly denying any intention to attack Fredericksfort.[5] Intense

---

[1]Dunbar to the Board of Trade, B. T. New Eng., Entry Bk. K, May 7, 1730.

[2]Letters from Dunbar to the Board of Trade, B. T., New Eng., Z: 217, 145; Petition from the Council and inhabitants of New Hampshire to be separated from Massachusetts, B. T. New Eng., Z: 218.

[3]Willis's Paper.

[4]Dunbar writes to the Board of Trade of his action in the affair, B. T., New Eng., Z: 145.

[5]Gov. Belcher to the Board of Trade, B. T. New Eng., Z: 155.

hostility to the surveyor prevailed, and his enemies employed agents to work for his removal. Dunbar had many friends, however, and, to the great mortification of Belcher, the post of Lieutenant Governor of New Hampshire was given to him, rather than to Belcher's own candidate.[1] On the other hand, the Privy Council settled the question of jurisdiction in favor of Massachusetts, and a garrison from the province was put in place of Dunbar's soldiers.[2]

Dunbar's letters are so taken up with boundary disputes and his ill treatment by the governor and by his enemies of Massachusetts, that very little is said about the experiments of the settlers in naval stores. Dunbar was not able to be on the spot, for any length of time, to superintend the production of stores, and the security of the settlers was constantly threatened by the Massachusetts proprietors, on the one hand, and the danger of Indian raids on the other. According to the deposition of one Samuel McCobb,[3] who was trying to establish his claim to some of the property granted by Dunbar, the reason for the failure of the settlement was that the land was poor and uncultivated, and the settlers from Ireland too poor and ignorant of methods of improving land to make a living off the soil. They depended solely on the sale of firewood, which they cut down and carried to Boston and other towns, until the murders and depredations of the Indians, in 1745, scattered the settlers and drove them westward, thus ending the attempt to produce stores on the Kennebec lands.

---

[1] B. T. New Eng., Entry Bk. K., letter from the Duke of Newcastle, March 5, 1731, recommending Dunbar. Palfrey, Vol. V, p. 568.

[2] Palfrey, Vol. V, p. 569.

[3] Dated October 23, 1772, Files of the State House, Boston, quoted by Johnston, "History of Bristol and Bremen."

PART II.

CHAPTER I.

THE ENCOURAGEMENT OFFERED TO IMPORTERS IN THE FORM OF BOUNTIES AND EXEMPTION FROM DUTIES.

Two circumstances rendered the supply of naval stores a problem of vital importance just at the opening of the eighteenth century. The first was the outbreak of the war of the Spanish Succession and the Grand Alliance of the naval powers against France, which required that the English fleet should be at its best in point of size and equipment. The second was the formation of the Stockholm Tar Company for the monopoly of trade in pitch and tar.

Great Britain bought practically her entire supply of those products from Sweden. The Swedish merchants, fully aware that their tar was the best in the world, perceived their opportunity to form an exceedingly profitable monopoly. They therefore proceeded to make regulations that no maker should sell to any other merchants, and that no ships, foreign or Swedish, should load any tar except for their account and by their order. By this means the company intended not only to set what prices they pleased, but, by ousting foreign shippers, to force English merchants to buy in English, instead of Swedish, ports, and pay freight. From the mercantilist point of view, this was a national as well as a commercial misfortune; for, as a writer of the day expressed it, "losing that trade was putting a number of ships out of employment, and, consequently, paying our neighbors for work, whilst our people were unemployed."[1] It was on this ground that complaint was first heard, but when the declaration of war with France led to the overhauling of the navy for the equipment of the fleet, and it was found that

---

[1] "Letter to a Member of Parliament concerning the Naval Stores Bill," 1720.

there was not sufficient pitch and tar in London for present use the situation called for immediate action.

In the spring of 1703, the Secretary of State wrote to Doctor Robinson, Her Majesty's envoy to Sweden, to see what were the prospects of obtaining from thence a supply on short notice. The reply of the envoy was of such a character that the Secretary had it copied out and given to several merchants "that they might see how much it was in the power of the king of Sweden to forward the fitting out of the Royal Navy of England or to keep it in harbour." In this letter,[1] Dr. Robinson informed Secretary Hedges that he had transmitted Her Majesty's letter to the King of Sweden. The latter had written on the 20th of March to the College of Commerce, at Stockholm, requesting them to give all due assistance to the English factors employed to buy up tar for Her Majesty's service, so that they might obtain for ready money what was due (apparently on contract) for the two former years, and what was desired for the present year.

Shortly after this, Dr. Robinson was informed that the directors of the tar trade had represented it to the king as a grievance that they should be obliged to deliver any pitch or tar for the English navy at Stockholm, when they could gain so much more advantage by carrying it to England and selling on their own account. Dr. Robinson then urged that the king's letter be complied with, at least for that one occasion; but the Tar Company proved incorrigible, and declared that they would export tar and pitch to England only on their own account, and at the market price fixed. This, said the envoy, was all that Her Majesty had to expect. It was reported that a good round sum had been offered to facilitate the matter, but without effect. From this it was quite evident that the directors of trade intended to monopolize the transport of all pitch and tar to England, as they had done for many years in the case of Holland, and that Her Majesty would consequently be forced to choose between buying at the directors' prices or seizing what

[1]"Letter to a Member of Parliament concerning the Naval Stores Bill."

they sent on the sea, or in port, and taking it at reasonable rates.

There were no other available European sources of supply. Courland and Finland were in the hands of the Swedes; Norway yielded very little tar, and that of a poor quality; and not much was to be got from Muscovy. Retaliation, by increasing the duties on Swedish tar, was a possible method of forcing down the Stockholm Company's prices, but the risk seemed too great, in view of the pressing needs of the navy. There were, however, the plantations in America, and it remained to be seen whether these could be depended upon to furnish supplies of proper quality and of sufficient quantity. Dr. Robinson wrote in his letter: "What difficulties there are in making and bringing it (tar) from New England, I am not acquainted with, but take it for granted England had better give one-third more for it from thence, than have it at such uncertainties, and in so precarious a manner from other countries."

The Board of Trade and all the merchants who had anything to do with importing colonial products were fully aware of the difficulties of which Dr. Robinson expressed his ignorance. The question had been fully discussed by the Board in their deliberations on the Dudley petition, which was still pending.[1] The chief obstacle to production was the scarcity and dearness of labor in the plantations; while the expense and danger incurred in transportation rendered competition with the Baltic countries out of the question, if the Navy continued to insist upon their policy of buying in the cheapest market. Another discouragement to importation was the inferior quality of American pitch and tar, by reason of the ignorance of the people of the proper methods of manufacture. Of course, it was not difficult to devise measures for obviating all these difficulties, but the government felt a reasonable hesitation about incurring the great expense which a serious and thorough-going attempt to promote the colonial manufacture of pitch and tar would involve. To the most liberal economists of the time, it appeared

[1] Cf. Part I, Ch. II, p. 29.

a profitable investment to devote national capital to the encouragement of such products as the government would otherwise be obliged to purchase from foreign powers and pay for in gold and silver. Joshua Gee, who a few years later gave the government the benefit of his views on economic policy, strongly advocated such expenditure, bringing forward as an example, the attention and pains which the Russian Czar, Peter the Great, devoted to developing the economic and industrial resources of his kingdom by a careful personal investigation of the industries of other nations, and by paying workmen to go to foreign countries to learn the best methods of the day.[1] Though somewhat niggardly in the matter of outlay, the Board of Trade had already gone so far as to send a commission to America to gather information about the prospects of supplying the navy from thence, and to instruct the planters in the methods of production in vogue in the north countries.[2]

They had also made inquiries, from time to time, of the navy contractors and the merchants trading to the plantations, with regard to the prices of colonial, as compared with Swedish, tar, and the relative expense of transportation. From the statistics sent in by the experts consulted, as they appear in the records, it is not easy to make an accurate comparison of the differences, because the reports do not in all cases state whether the price is given in New England money or in pounds sterling, or whether the estimate refers to goods delivered in England or at the place of shipment. Further, the capacity of the Swedish and the American barrel differed, the former containing from thirty to thirty-two gallons, while the New Englanders reckoned only from eight to nine gallons to their barrel. By piecing together these statistics, however, some idea can be got of the differences of price upon which the Board based their opinion of what premium would be necessary to counteract the expenses of production and transportation, so that the merchants might

---

[1] "Gee's Memorial," B. T. Plantations General, Bundle L, No. 24.
[2] Cf. Part I, Ch. I, p. 9.

be induced to engage in the regular importation of colonial stores.[1]

From about 1690 to 1700 the prices which the navy paid for tar ranged from £6 to £12 sterling, or over, per last (12 barrels); pitch from £6 to £10 15s. per ton, the fluctuations being due to war. To what height the Swedish prices rose at the time of the Stockholm monopoly, does not appear in the lists, but Mr. Gee, in a later discussion of this monopoly,[2] says that the company had raised the price of tar to nearly three pounds per barrel. Haynes quotes current prices in London, in November, 1703, at forty shillings per barrel for tar, and fifty shillings per barrel for pitch.[3] The prices offered by merchants trading to the plantations or by contractors, are lower than might be expected, but as they are frequently given by competing bidders, on presumption of government encouragement, and represent an inferior quality of product, the cheapness is more apparent than real. New York tar had been offered by Colonel Fletcher, in 1693, at 12 pounds per last, when the Navy was buying at 11 pounds 12 shillings and 6 pence.[4] At the hearing of contractors before the Board of Trade, in March, 1694,[5] there was one proposal to supply tar at £2 13s. per last (New England barrels), which would amount to about £10 for a last of Swedish barrels. Allan and Evance offered as their prices for goods delivered in England,—tar at £13 4s. per last, pitch at £25 per ton.[6] Slye, of Maryland, would contract for tar delivered in the province at £5 4s. per last; pitch at £4 16s.; other stores in proportion.[7] In 1699, Bridger and Holland sent over from New England an offer to supply tar, after two years, at £7 16s. sterling, per last, delivered in New England. In the same year, Governor Bello-

---

[1] Cf. Price List, Appendix A.
[2] Memorial to the Board of Trade, B. T. Plants. Gen., L : 24.
[3] Memorandum of Haynes' proposals, B. T., New Eng., N : 3.
[4] Cf. Price List, Appendix A.
[5] Ibid.
[6] Proposals offered by Evance compared with Slye's prices, B. T. Plants. Gen., C : 23.
[7] Ibid.

mont quoted the current prices of Carolina tar as £4 4s. (probably sterling);[1] but Carolina tar was made from knots and rough pieces of pine wood, and not from prepared trees, so that the quality was inferior to European tar. In answer to inquiries as to the charge for freight, Mr. Bridger informed the Board that the rate on tar from New England would be about £4 per ton in peace, and £6 in war.[2] Haynes calculated freight at from £6 to £7 per last (about 2 tons).[3] The Virginia estimate was higher, being £6 in peace and £12 in war.

In October, 1703, Secretary Hedges notified the Board of Trade of Her Majesty's command, that they should consider the possibility of procuring stores from New England and the other plantations in America, and submit their opinion of ways and means to the Privy Council at their next meeting.[4] In order to comply with this request, the Board invited fresh proposals for contracts, and suggestions for stimulating the trade in stores. Mr. Bridger sent in an offer to supply 5,000 barrels of tar and pitch in five years, at 20 shillings per cwt. for pitch, and 30 shillings per barrel for tar (30 gallons to the barrel), delivered at Deptford, providing Her Majesty would advance £6,000 in specie at the signing of the contract, £4,000 toward the second year, and so on in proportion; besides providing convoy to and from the plantations.[5] Richard Haynes and Company proposed to deliver at Portsmouth, Bristol or London, two years from the date of contract, 1,500 barrels of pitch and tar (Stockholm gauge), at 50 shillings per barrel for pitch, and 40 shillings for tar, the current London prices; and in peace, "for so much less as they should find the freight lower; provided that their annual importation for seven years be customs free, and taken off their hands and paid for two months after deliv-

[1] Gov. Bellomont to the Board of Trade, B. T. New Eng. F: 25.

[2] Bridger to the Board of Trade, B. T. New Eng, O: 5.

[3] Haynes to the Board of Trade, March, 1700, B. T. Plants. Gen., D: 18.

[4] Secretary Hedges to the Board of Trade, B. T. New Eng., N: 1.

[5] Bridger's proposals to the Board of Trade, Nov., 1703, B. T. New Eng., N: 2.

ery, at the prices mentioned." The freight at that date was estimated at the exceedingly high rate of 25 shillings per barrel and insurance with convoy at about nine per cent.[1] Messrs. Mason and Oursel, after having consulted several merchants, reported to the Board that the opinion prevailed that considerable pitch and tar could be furnished from the plantations; but that the merchants were "tender of engaging in any contract lest they should be under a necessity of disappointing Her Majesty or ruining their families, for the following reasons." These reasons are worth quoting in full, as an epitome of the merchant's position : [2]

1. "If the rumors of such a contract spread abroad prices would immediately rise greatly, we being under the absolute necessity of buying.   2. Though we should order our factors to get us supplies, the task would be difficult, because land is generally particular men's property, which we cannot expect to purchase.   3. Little land remains to the Crown near the sea or any river, and the best lands are now in New Hampshire and Maine, which are now embroiled by the Indians.   4. By the time due provision can be made for making tar, peace may be made, and Her Majesty be supplied otherwise much cheaper. 5. We must pay to seamen double what Her Majesty pays.   6. Shipping being scarce, and we under necessity of sending, an extraordinary freight will be exacted.   7. We fear to depend on convoys, there having been so many instances of serious delays by being blown off the coast." In view of this hesitation, of the merchants to make contracts, Mason and Oursel suggested that it would be better to employ merchants, whose credit was good, to purchase stores on commission, to Her Majesty's account, through factors in the plantations.

The Lords of Trade forwarded all the above proposals and suggestions to the Privy Council with their own report.   In this they reviewed the Dudley case and their inability to come to

---

[1] Richard Haynes's proposals, Nov. 1703, B. T. New Eng., N: 3.
[2] Memorial from Messrs. Mason and Oursel, Nov. 11, 1703, B. T. New Eng., N: 4.

terms with the petitioners, and expressed their opinion that, in view of the disadvantages which the merchants enumerated, very little could be expected through private enterprise; so that the only method of promoting trade would be to induce the government to bear some part of the expense, by offering a premium to importers to compensate for the dearness of freight.[1] A second report sent in to the Privy Council five months later, at the Queen's request, offers no new suggestions, but repeats the opinion of the Board, that, as all the plantations together could not, under the existing conditions, supply enough stores for the navy, some provision for a bounty was desirable.[2] Whereupon, Secretary Hedges wrote to inquire what premium, in their opinion, might be offered with least burden to the public.[3] The Board consulted Mr. Bridger, who was then in London. He suggested 10 shillings a barrel (4 pounds a ton) for pitch and tar, as sufficient to induce the merchants to venture on importation and the colonies to apply themselves to the production of those commodities.[4] The Board, accordingly, recommended that 3 pounds per ton be offered by way of experiment for three years, beginning in January, 1705, and that the duty be removed, as a further encouragement.[5].

On the 18th of December, 1704, the Secretary informed the Lords of Trade that the House of Commons had that day given leave for a bill to be brought in to encourage the importation of naval stores from the plantations.[6] Therefore, in accordance with a command from the Privy Council, the Board of Trade drafted a bill which was passed by Parliament early in 1705, to go into effect in January of that year and to continue in force nine years. By this act[7] provision was made for the encourage-

---

[1] B. T. New Eng., N: 4.

[2] Report of Board of Trade, B. T. New Eng., Entry Book E., March 18, 1704.

[3] Secretary Hedges to the Board of Trade, B. T. New Eng., O: 36.

[4] Proposal by Bridger, B. T. New Eng., O: 38.

[5] Board of Trade to Secretary Hedges, B. T. Plants. Gen., Ent. Bk. A, June 23, 1704.

[6] Secretary Hedges to the Board of Trade, B. T. Plants. Gen., G: 24.

[7] 3 and 4 Anne, c. 9.

ment, not only of pitch, tar and allied products, but also for masts and heavy ship timber. The preamble, which explains the objects of the act, contains, in a nutshell, the current theory of the normal commercial relation between the mother-country and the colonies. It reads:

"*Whereas* the Royal Navy and the Navigation of England wherein under God the Wealth and Safety and Strength of this Kingdom is so much concerned, depends on the due supply of Stores necessary for the same, which being now brought mostly from Foreign Parts in Foreign Shipping at exorbitant and Arbitrary Rates to the great Prejudice and Discouragement of the Trade and Navigation of this Kingdom, may be provided in a more certain and beneficial Manner from Her Majesty's own Dominions; And Whereas her Majesty's Colonies and Plantations in America were first settled and are still maintained and protected at a great Expense to the Treasure of this Kingdom with a Design to render them as useful as may be to England, and the Labor and Industry of the People there profitable to themselves; And in regard the said Colonies and Plantations by the vast Tracts of Land therein lying near the Sea and upon navigable Rivers may commodiously afford great Quantities of all Sorts of Naval Stores if due Encouragement be given for carrying on so great and advantageous an Undertaking, which will likewise tend not only to the further Imployment and Increase of English Shipping and Seamen, but also to the Inlarging in a great Measure the Trade and Vent of the Woolen and other Manufactures and Commodities of this Kingdom and of other Her Majesty's Dominions, in Exchange for such Naval Stores which are now purchased from Foreign Countries with Money or Bullion. And for enabling Her Majesty's Subjects in the said Colonies and Plantations to continue to make due and sufficient Returns in the course of their Trade, Be it therefore enacted, etc."

The rates of premium granted on stores imported directly from any of the plantations in any ships manned according to the requirements of the law were as follows:

For good and merchantable tar, 4 pounds per ton (each ton to contain 8 barrels of 31½ gallons each).
For good and merchantable pitch, 4 pounds per ton (each ton to contain 20 gross hundreds in 8 barrels).
For hemp, water-rotted, bright and clean, 6 pounds per ton.
For all masts, yards and bowsprits, 1 pound per ton (allowing 40

foot to each ton, girt measure, according to the customary way of measuring round bodies).

The premiums were to be awarded by the principal officers of the navy, who were empowered to make out bills payable in course, and elaborate provision was made for certificates of evidence that the stores were actually of the growth of the plantations. The imports were to be subject to the same regulations as imported sugar, tobacco, etc., *i. e.*, they were included among the enumerated commodities whose importation was restricted to the home market.

The effect of the publication of the act by the governors of the several colonies was felt immediately. The petitions of Bridger and of the merchants and traders to New England, that a person be sent over to teach the people how to prepare pitch and tar properly, led to the appointment of a surveyor of the woods.[1] The Massachusetts Assembly passed an act regulating the "assize of casks" for pitch, tar and turpentine, and providing for the appointment of viewers and gaugers to examine the size of the casks, to see that they were completely filled with tar or pitch of the proper quality, and, in general, to prevent frauds and deceits.[2] Governor Seymour, of Maryland, wrote in August, 1706, that Her Majesty's favor in admitting stores had been very thankfully received by the inhabitants of that province, many of whom had large fields jaded with tobacco, but which might be very proper for hemp, the sowing and reaping of which would be no hindrance to the tobacco culture. The Assembly, he said, had enacted a law that hemp and flax should be current in part payment for debt. Maryland could not supply masts and bowsprits, but there were great quantities of pine woods, and many of the people were aiming at pitch and tar, though greatly handicapped by their lack of

---

[1] Memorial from Mr. Bridger, March 16, 1705, B. T. Plants. Gen., H: 4 and petition from merchants and traders to New England, B. T. New Eng., P: 35. See Part II, Ch. II.
[2] Acts and Laws of H. M. Prov. of Mass. Bay, (Edit. 1742,) p. 130.

skill in preparing the trees.[1]   The Board of Trade wrote back that Mr. Bridger, the surveyor, would give them any instructions they required.

The products imported from New England the first year under the new act, amounting to 6,191 barrels of tar, 647 of pitch, 1,145 of turpentine, and 90 of rosin,[2] were, necessarily, of somewhat inferior quality, because they had been prepared before Bridger's arrival.   The latter wrote that he hoped the authorities would be lenient in awarding the bounty, on account of the stores having been made without instructions; he would engage that future importations should equal those from the East Country.   He said that the interest of the New Englanders in the outcome of this first venture was intense ; that everything was stopped to await the result ; and he urged that if the people were disappointed in receiving the bounty on their first load, they would not try again, but would return to spinning and sheep-raising.[3]

On receipt of this warning, the Board of Trade recommended to the Lord High Treasurer that the undertaking should be encouraged by payment of the full premium, without too much scruple about the quality.   They also called a conference of the Navy Board to consider Bridger's communications,[4] and after the consultation reported the results to the Privy Council. The Navy said that they must distinguish between their own interests and those of England.   They were obliged by their instructions to buy stores where they could find them cheapest, and they had, therefore, usually preferred the pitch and tar of Sweden.   They had already made their contracts for the ensuing year,[5] a part of the supplies being expected from New

---

[1]Gov. Seymour to the Board of Trade, June 12, 1706, B. T. Md. Docts., H: 22D.

[2]Mr. Bridger to the Board of Trade, B. T., New Eng., Q: 53.

[3]Bridger to the Board of Trade, B. T. New Eng., Q: 52.

[4]Board of Trade to the Lord High Treasurer, B. T. New Eng., Entry Bk. F., December 6, 1706.

[5]It appears that Swedish prices had fallen in consequence of the act. B. T. Plants. Gen., Entry Bk., D., March 21, 1711, Report of the Board of Trade.

England. They approved of promoting importation from the plantations, because the greater the number of competitors, the cheaper would be the price; and, provided the plantations produced pitch and tar as cheaply as other places, they were willing to give them due encouragement. In regard to the present shipping, the act required the commodities to be good and merchantable, in order to receive the premium, but in case these first importations were really serviceable, even if not quite up to the Swedish standard, they had no objection to cautioning the customs officers against being too severe in their judgment.[1]

In January of the following year (1707), the Board of Trade received a letter from Governor Dudley, in which he expressed his great interest in the results of the Naval Stores Act. He reported that more tar and turpentine had been sent in the last fleet than for some years, and he hoped that, if this tar proved acceptable, it would come to be a staple of the country.[2] Mr. Bridger wrote, at the same time, that the people were generally inclined to promote the raising of stores and had given him leave to move, next assize, any law he thought good, in view of that end.[3]

In order to ascertain exactly what were the effects of the bounty, the Board of Trade sent for statistics of the importations from the plantations and the bounties awarded since the act went into effect.[4] The desired reports were sent in, but I have not quoted them here because the most interesting comparisons are to be got from lists prepared at a later date, covering a period of fifteen years and recording for each year the importations from Sweden, the rest of Europe, and the plantations.[5] From these more exhaustive statistics it appears that the importation of tar had increased very slowly from 1701 to

---

[1] Navy Board to the Board of Trade, B. T., New Eng., Q: 58, and Memorandum of Meeting, B. T. Journal, fol. 17.

[2] Gov. Dudley to the Board of Trade, B. T., New Eng., R: 27.

[3] Mr. Bridger to the Board Trade, B. T., New Eng., R: 29.

[4] Account of importations sent by Chas. Davenant, B. T., New Eng., R: 10.

[5] See tables, Appendix B. B. T. Trade Papers, No. 23, pp. 105-108.

the passing of the act, but in the last year before the bounty was offered, only 872 barrels of pitch and tar had been brought from the plantations, as over against 42,856 from Sweden and 17,797 from the rest of Europe.   The next year's account shows a falling off of over 10,000 barrels for Sweden, 3,000 for the rest of Europe, and a gain of 1,474 barrels for the plantations. In 1706, the importation from Sweden decreased by over 8,000 barrels; that from the rest of Europe was only half that of 1705, while the plantations gained 4,000 barrels.   It should be noted that the total importation had decreased during the last three years, *i. e.*, since the outbreak of the war with France.   In 1707, the Swedish importation was about the same as in 1706, while the plantation figures rose to the highest point reached in any year until after the renewal of the act in 1714, and exceeded the rest of Europe by over three thousand.   The year 1708 showed a very slight increase for Sweden and the rest of Europe, and a falling off of more than 3,000 barrels for the plantations.

Bridger, in a letter received March 13, 1708, accounts for this decrease, by saying that the failure of the Navy to pay the premiums according to the act had discouraged the people from buying stores and that they preferred to send other goods at greater loss.[1]   The Board wrote back that Bridger must be mistaken about the refusal of the Navy to pay the premium, for certificates of the good quality of the stores had certainly been issued at the custom house; but they would investigate the matter.[2]   When questioned, the custom house officers reported that 588 tons, 7 barrels, 15 gallons of tar; and 643 tons, 12 hundred weight, one-quarter, 5 pounds of pitch had received certificates for the premium up to November 29, 1707.[3] This would amount to more than 12,223 barrels, counting 2 cwt. to the barrel.   The total importation of pitch and tar from December 25, 1704 ,to December 25, 1707, if the table can be trusted, was 18,459 barrels; so that something like six thousand barrels must have

---

[1] Mr. Bridger to the Board of Trade, B. T. New Eng., R: 53.
[2] Board of Trade to Mr. Bridger, B. T. New Eng., R: Entry for July 7, 1708.
[3] Memorandum of Custom House Report, B. T. Plants. Gen. I: 46.

failed to receive certificates. On making inquiries whether the premium had been paid, the Board learned from the merchants, that they had received bills from the Navy Office "payable in course," but carrying no interest, as most of the Navy bills did after six months; so that the importers would not receive above two-thirds of what the act allowed.[1] There was, apparently, no separate fund established from which the premiums were paid, and the annoyance of the Navy Board that they should be obliged to pay the importers, added to their half-hearted sympathy with the project, probably led to the tardy payment of which the merchants continued to complain. On the other hand, the preference of the colonies for other commodities of trade, and their increasing interest in woolen manufactures and the lumber business combined to discourage the production of naval stores, at the least sign of the abatement of profits.

In February, 1710, Bridger wrote[2] that the merchants in New England were a trifle more encouraged by what the Board had written to Governor Dudley with regard to the importance of the trade, and that they had met several times and agreed on certain suggestions which they desired to have carried out. He was very much discouraged in his attempts to reason with them, by the behavior of Mr. Mico, who had been very hostile to the surveyor in his efforts to prevent the destruction of the woods by the loggers.[3] This busybody had attended the meetings and undone Bridger's work, by seeking to dissuade the merchants from having anything more to do with naval stores. The memorial which the merchants of Boston and Portsmouth finally drew up, suggested as remedies for their grievances :[4]

(1) That the premium should be paid in a short set time, and funds granted. (This last probably means that the government should make

---

[1] Report of Board of Trade, B. T. Plants. Gen. Entry Bk. D., March 21, 1711.
[2] Mr. Bridger to the Board of Trade, Feb. 1710, B. T. New Eng., S: 89.
[3] Cf. Part II, Ch. II.
[4] Representation from Merchants of Boston and Portsmouth, B. T. New Eng., S: 61.

a special appropriation for the payment of the bounty, instead of depending upon the convenience of the Navy Board.)[1]

(2) That the act be extended in time, on account of wars and other discouragements.

(3) That all stores should be taken off their hands at the following rates above the premium:

Tar at 18 shillings per bbl., or £10 16s. per last.
Pitch at 18 shillings per bbl., or £6 12s. per last.
Rosin at 16 shillings per bbl.

(4) That suitable convoys be provided.

(5) That all stores be sealed by the surveyor, and that certificates be given of their fitness to be accepted for the bounty. (The object of the last request was to prevent loss of freight, in case the stores were rejected after transportation.)

The export of pitch and tar from New England continued to decrease, but the occupation of the people with the Indian Wars may have accounted for this in a large measure. The act would have expired in 1714, and Bridger wrote to urge its renewal, insisting that when peace was made, the people would undoubtedly make large quantities of pitch and tar.[2] The Board seems to have been satisfied on the whole with the working of the bounty act, for in their "Report on Naval Stores," presented to the Privy Council in the spring of 1711, they expressed their judgment that plantation tar might now be sold as cheaply as that from the North Countries; and, even if dearer, it was to the interest of the nation to have it from America, since it could be paid for in woolens and other manufactures, instead of in money. The former objections to the burning quality of American tar had been removed, and traders said that it was now as good and fit for rope as that from Stockholm.[3] The act was accordingly renewed, in 1714, for eleven years,[4] but no change was made in the method of paying the premiums. The

---

[1] Cf. also, Banister's "Essay on the Trade of New England." B. T. New Eng., V: 9.

[2] Report of Board of Trade, B. T. Plants. Gen. Entry Bk. D., March 21, 1711.

[3] Ibid.

[4] 12 Anne, c. 9.

continuance of the bounty gave a fresh impetus to importation and the amount of pitch and tar recorded rose from 4,825 barrels, in 1713, to 82,084 in 1718,—an increase of 77,259 barrels in five years.

The encouragement had not proved so stimulating to the importation of ship-timber, although the reports show a fairly steady increase. The largest number of great masts brought over from 1701 to the passing of the first bounty act was 81, in 1703, when the total importation of great masts was 710. The maximum import from the plantations between 1705 and 1715 was 261, in a year when 1,981 masts were brought from Sweden and the rest of Europe. Very few "middle" and "small" masts were brought from America,[1] and the north country timber continued to be much cheaper. On the other hand, it was constantly asserted by the surveyor, the governors and the merchants, that the supply of New England would be boundless if the waste of the loggers could be stopped, and the Board of Trade were informed by those whom they consulted, that, although discredited by the Navy Board (who seem to have been prejudiced in their judgment), New England masts were elsewhere reckoned fully as good as Rupia, and many as good as Riga, masts. Therefore, having successfully provided for the importation of pitch and tar, the Board turned their attention to the further encouragement of timber. In 1711, they had, in consequence of some suggestions of Governor Dudley, sounded the Admiralty on the advisability of offering a premium on spars and boards as well as on other stores.[2] The Admiralty, having consulted the Navy Board, said they had no objection, but could not advise what premium would be proper; while the Navy protested that such a bounty ought not to be paid by them, but by the Custom House, or in some other way : they could buy cheaper from the East Country.[3]

---

[1] See table, Appendix B.
[2] The Board of Trade to Secretary Burchett, B. T. New Eng. Entry Bk. G., Jan. 5, 1711.
[3] Navy Board to Board of Trade, B. T. New Eng. T: 17.

Nothing further seems to have been done about the matter until 1715, when Colonel Vaughan presented some "considerations on the province of New Hampshire "[1]—the chief source of the mast supply—in which he recommended that the importation of masts and other stores be encouraged by the removal of the duty. The Board consulted several merchants as to the annual supply which could be expected from the plantations, and as to the best means of encouragement. Mr. Cummings computed that about 150,000 deals and planks, 100,000 hogshead, and 100,000 barrel staves might be imported annually; larger timber he thought too bulky to be profitable. He held that the only way to encourage importation would be to remove the duty and allow twenty shillings for every ship-load.[2] Samson and Sheafe estimated that 30,000 deals could be produced in New England, beyond the Navy contracts and besides a supply for New England and the other plantations, if encouraged by the removal of the duty. They gave as the first cost of one-and-a-quarter-inch boards, in New England, 50 shillings per hundred (1000 feet), and the freight 4 pounds per hundred.[3] In view of the enormous increase in price which such a rate of freight occasioned, certain merchants petitioned that the proposed bill for taking off the duty from timber be passed if possible during the present session of Parliament (the spring of 1715).[4]

This was not accomplished, and in January of the following year a further memorial was received from the merchants, in which they petitioned that "All duties payable inwards on tar, pitch, rosin, turpentine, potash, hemp, flax, plank, boards, masts, oares, staves, and all other sorts of wood (except that used for dyeing and drugs), from any of the plantations, be taken off; second, that whereas the difference of freight between the plantations and the East Country was as 15 to 45, a bounty equivalent thereto should be given to the importer, and

---

[1] Col. Vaughan, to the Board of Trade, B. T. New Eng. V: 44.
[2] Memorial from Mr. Cummings, B. T. New Eng. V: 46.
[3] Calculation by Samson and Sheafe, B. T. New Eng. V: 47.
[4] Memorial from merchants, B. T. New Eng. V: 58.

that all bounty bills be put on the same footing for payment as contract bills; thirdly, that in war all ships should have a convoy and the sailors be exempt from impressment during such voyage out and home."

If these provisions were made, they hoped to be able to supply stores at the following rates, exclusive of the bounty : tar, at 16 shillings per barrel; pitch, at 10 shillings per cwt.; turpentine, at 14 shillings, 6 pence per cwt.; rosin, at 18 shillings per cwt.; masts, according to prices in the navy contract. To strengthen their case they enclosed several certificates from ship-builders, testifying to the good quality of American masts;[1] and they further proposed that the governors of the colonies be instructed to cause every manufacturer to brand his name into each barrel of tar, pitch or turpentine. Jeremiah Dummer advised the granting of a bounty of 20 shillings per ton on all timber, in addition to the removal of the duty, in order to render importation more certain and to procure larger supplies. The bounty on pitch and tar had reduced prices nearly one-half, and he was confident that timber would fall in the same way, so that the nation would be the gainer, rather than the loser, by the bounty.[2] The agents of Carolina and merchants trading there, to whom the Board also applied for information, reported an export of more than 20,000 barrels of the pitch and tar of that province, which was pronounced by rope-makers little inferior to Stockholm products. Carolina produced timber of various sorts, but the freight and duty made exportation unprofitable. They recommended that hemp be made duty free, since the bounty had not been sufficient to encourage production. Several further memorials were presented to the Board, all recommending the removal of duties on timber.

The Navy, when asked their opinion about the advisability of taking off the duty on stores, reported in their usual non-committal manner that they were not able to judge in the matter ;

[1] Memorial from New England merchants, and certificates of quality of New England masts, B. T. New Eng. V: 99, 100.

[2] Mr. Dummer to the Board of Trade, February 25, 1716. B. T. New Eng., V: 124.

a very inconsiderable quantity of the pitch and tar imported from the colonies had been bought for the use of the Navy, in proportion to the expense incurred by them. The premiums, amounting to £80,000, had been a great clog to the Navy and no advantage; and if any more bounties were granted, some other provision for payment ought to be devised.[1] They sent to the Board of Trade a statement of the amount of their purchases of plantation stores from 1713 to 1717, and the amount of bounty paid.[2]

Total spent in premiums, £90,544 7s. 5d. Total amount of stores bought : Pitch, 2,398 bbls.; tar, 4,438 bbls. The report states that a great many stores were imported in these years, for which the proprietors brought no certificates from the custom house, and so could not receive the premium.

A great many complaints reached the Board of Trade that the importers were so keen about getting the bounty that the packing had been carelessly done, or else frauds had been purposely practiced to increase the weight of the stores.   In March, 1718, a circular letter was therefore sent to the governors of the plantations informing them of the poor quality of the tar and pitch lately imported, the tar being full of water, and the pitch mixed with sand and dirt for weight; so that certificates had been refused at the custom house. The governors

---

[1] Navy Board to Secretary Burchett, B. T. New Eng., V: 145.
[2] Account of premiums paid for naval stores by the Navy, B. T. Plants. Gen. K: 121.

	1713.	1714.	1715.	1716.	1717.
	£. s. d.	£. s. d.	£. s. d.	£. s.d.	£. s.d
Premiums,	5,783-19-10	6,860-8-10	10,135-10-9	27,410-7-9	40,354-0-3
Pitch,....	....	... ...	715 bbls.	75 bbls.	1,608 bbls.
Tar,......	. ...	....	665 "	....	3,773 "
Pitch, ...	....	....	£11-0-0	£9-0 0	£7-10-0 ton
	....	....	9-0-0	....	6-10-0
Tar,........	....	....	12-0-0	....	11-10-0 last
	....	....	11-0-0	....	11- 0-0

were directed to warn the people to take precautions in the future, for premiums could not be allowed on such stores.[1]

There seems to have been some talk of discontinuing the bounty, for a number of merchants who had heard rumors of such intention entered a strong protest, in which they enlarged on the good effects which the act had produced in the increase of importation, the great reduction in the price of pitch and tar, and the increase of exports of British manufactures. The merchants said that they themselves had, in consequence of the encouragement, gone to the expense of sending over workmen and utensils for improving the stores; and if now the bounty were taken off, the Swedes would regain their monopoly and again set what prices they pleased, to the ruin of the English traders.[2] From other sources the government was continually reminded of the bad policy of depending on the northern powers. The bounty act remained in force, but Parliament added a clause to 5 Geo. I., c. 11, by which it was enacted that, on account of the complaints made by the Navy of the poor quality of the pitch and tar recently imported from America, after September 29, 1719, no certificate should be granted until such pitch and tar be free from dross and pronounced "clean, good, merchantable and well-conditioned." The officers of the customs were required to examine the stores before making out any certificates.

In the meantime, the northern war of Russia, Denmark and Saxony, against Sweden, (1701-1721) had seriously interrupted the Baltic trade. Sweden had laid a new duty of nearly 25 per cent. on iron, which caused great distress among British iron merchants; the Danes had raised the price of boards from $8 to $9 (the rix dollar equalled 2 shillings, 2¾ pence) per 100; and Finland, the great tar-producing district, had fallen into the hands of Russia.[3] The exigencies and uncertainties of the war,

---

[1] Copy of circular letter to the governors of the plantations. B. T. Plants. Gen. Entry Bk. E, March 5, 1718.
[2] Petition of merchants trading to New England, Virginia and Carolina, B. T. New Eng., W: 38.
[3] "Letter to a Member of Parliament," 1720.

therefore, made it advisable to continue the policy of encouraging the importation of the products for which England depended on the northern crowns. In December, 1718, Joshua Gee recommended that a bounty be granted on bar and cast iron from the plantations, and that timber, boards and staves be let in free of duty.[1] The merchants were invited to wait on the Ministry at the Board of Trade and to express their views on these suggestions. They represented, first, that the proposed measure would at least lower the prices and lessen the imports of Danish and Swedish commodities, and they stated that 20,000 tons of foreign iron were required annually, to carry on their manufactures; secondly, that the plantation trade in these products would double the navigation, and would not only be an additional employment to English ship-builders, as well as to sailors and seamen, but it would increase the consumption of provisions. "As our navigation increases," argued these exponents of mercantilism, " that of Sweden and Denmark must, of course, sink." Lastly, they said, ships that were disappointed of their cargo, in years when the tobacco and sugar crops fell short, would no longer be forced to return dead-freighted, or to lie over for the whole season, as often transpired.[2]

After a great many meetings, in which it was satisfactorily demonstrated that it would be a great advantage to the kingdom to be supplied from the plantations and very much enlarge the export of woolen and other manufactures, a motion was made to bring a bill into the House for the accomplishment of those ends. Such a bill passed the Commons in 1719,[3] but with the addition of a clause forbidding the manufacture in the plantations of any iron wares made from sows, pigs or bars. The House of Lords added another clause forbidding "the erection of forges for making sows, pigs or cast iron into bars or rod iron." In a later memorial,[4] (October 27, 1721), Mr. Gee says

[1] "Joshua Gee's Account of Trade for Iron and Timber, with the Northern Crowns," B. T. Plants. Gen., Entry Bk. E., Dec. 31, 1718.
[2] "Letter to a Member of Parliament."
[3] Ibid.
[4] B. T. Plants. Gen., L: 24.

he fears that these clauses were " thrust in by the private views of some iron-masters who had not consideration enough to think of the true interest of their country." Whatever the origin of the clauses, the result of passing the act would have been, as the author of "A Letter to a Member of Parliament" put it, that no smith in the plantation could have made so much as a bolt, spike or nail; the iron works and ship-building would have been ruined. There was some opposition, also, to the importation of timber from the colonies. "The fondness of some people to keep in the old track," wrote Gee,[1] "has caused them to send their emissaries about and fill gentlemen with the notion that if we were supplied with boards and timber from America, our Royal Navy would be deprived of a sufficient supply of masts ; which pretenses have no shadow of reason in them, for it is well known that the whole supply of the Royal Navy rarely exceeds the number of 300 trees in a year for masts. Now what are 300 trees out of a forest 14 to 15 miles long and 300 to 400 miles broad?" There was timber enough in Maine, New Hampshire and Massachusetts to supply all Europe; and as to the objections urged against supplying other nations with materials for their navies, Mr. Gee very sensibly argued that, if England did not supply them, the Dutch would sell them East Country oak. Besides, there was no more profitable merchandise than timber, which on account of its bulk employed the greatest number of ships and sailors with very small expenditure of national capital. It was this sort of trade which had bred Denmark and Norway so many sailors and enabled them to fit out their navies. The clauses restraining manufacture killed the bill of 1719, for "the better-disposed" urged that the measure be dropped for that session.[2]

But the arguments of Mr. Gee prevailed a year or two later, and in 1722 another general naval stores act was passed,[3] which was a sort of revised version of the preceding acts, correcting

[1] B. T. Plants. Gen., L: 24.
[2] "Letter to a Member of Parliament;" and Macpherson's "Annals of Commerce," Vol. III, page 72.
[3] 8 Geo. I, c. 12.

them in such particulars as experience had shown them open
to criticism, and adding some new provisions.   Section 1 related to the production of hemp, the previous encouragement
of which had not proved successful.   In view of the large tracts
of land in the plantations and in Scotland, lying near the sea and
on navigable rivers, upon which hemp might be profitably cultivated if sufficient encouragement were given, it was enacted
that the bounty of 6 pounds given by the previous act for every
ton of hemp water-rotted, bright and clean, should be continued from the expiration of the act, 12 Anne, during a term of
16 years; and that after June 24, 1722, all such hemp lawfully
imported should be free from all duties and customs.   Section 2
removed the duties from all sorts of woods, plank and timber
imported directly from the plantations in accordance with the
navigation laws.   Section 3 reserved for the royal navy the
right of pre-emption of all hemp imported under this act.   Section 4 made an important change in the regulation of the premium on pitch and tar.   It reads:

"And whereas a premium was given for tar (3 and 4 Anne), continued by 12 Anne, and provision made against frauds by 5 Geo. I. c. 2;
and whereas the tar imported from the plantations has hitherto been
found to retain an hot and thick quality whereby it is not so fit for
cordage as the East Country tar; for remedy thereof, be it enacted
that from and after September 29, 1724, no certificate be made by the
Officer of Customs for tar imported, *** nor bill granted by the Commissioners of the Navy to entitle the importer to the premium, unless a
certificate from the Governor, Lieut. Governor, Collector of Customs and Navy Officers or any two of them, do express that such tar
was made from green trees in the manner hereby prescribed; That is
to say, that when such trees were fit to bark, the bark thereof was
stripped eight feet or thereabouts up from the root of each tree, a slip
of the bark of about four inches in breadth having been left on the side
of each tree; and that each tree, after having been so barked, had
stood during one year at least and was not cut down for making of
tar."

The news of the requirement of conformity to the rules prescribed by the act caused dismay and consternation among the
merchants, who lost no time in entering a protest against such

a restriction. In May, 1723, a memorial was received by the Board of Trade from the London merchants, informing them that the inhabitants of the plantations were mostly ignorant of the proper methods of preparing tar and had refused to prepare trees at all, if they could not get the premium except by the new rules. The merchants prayed that some skillful person be sent over to instruct them.[1] As a matter of fact, this was precisely what Bridger was supposed to have done, but it had doubtless been impossible for him to give personal instruction to any extent; and when he had caused printed rules to be distributed, the people had refused to abandon their old methods unless the superiority of the new way should be demonstrated before their eyes.

The rapid increase in exportation from the plantations had tended to confirm the people in their disposition to let well enough alone; so that the act of 1721 served effectually to suppress what little enthusiasm the original bounty provision had aroused. At any rate, the fact that the development of shipbuilding and woolen manufacture, together with the rapid increase in the carrying trade in what served as the staples of New England, was rendering the inhabitants less likely to be dependent on the development of the naval stores trade, was enough to make the disappointment less serious to the producers.

The merchant-importers' point of view was quite different. In the next year (1724), another petition was made by certain "importers and dealers in tar," insisting that the prescribed rules were impracticable in the plantations, and that tar could not be made from green trees.[2] They begged that the premium be continued on tar made by the old method, which had already been proved practicable, as enclosed certificates of the goodness of American tar from ten ship-wrights testified.[3] If the plantations stopped making tar, as they certainly would if the rules

---

[1] Memorial of merchants trading to the Plantations, B. T. Plants. Gen., 1.: 44.

[2] Ibid. [3] B. T. Plants. Gen., 1.: 54.

were insisted upon, Russian prices would immediately rise to what they had been before the plantation trade had lowered them, and the nation would again be forced to pay high rates in ready money. The price of the best Finland tar at that date was compared with plantation prices.[1]

Finland tar, per barrel, (first cost)...........	£ 0–4–0
Freight....................................	4
Freight, packing, etc........	3
Total................................	£0–11–0
American tar, per barrel (first cost).........	£ 0–7–0
Freight in peace..........................	8–0
Leakage, etc..............................	3–0
Premium..................................	1–6
Total....................	£0–19–6

The comparison shows that the American price had been reduced to about the normal price of north country tar in 1703; while competition had forced Russian prices down so that Finland tar was still cheaper than American; but as the merchants pointed out, the chief utility of the plantation importation was to prevent the rise of prices by monopoly. Sweden must have been watching the effects of the English naval stores legislation with keen interest, for, by the treaty with Russia at the close of the Baltic war in 1721, she had regained Finland, and was only waiting for an opportunity to recover her lost trade in pitch and tar.[2] Any relaxation by the British government of their encouragement of colonial stores would react in favor of Swedish importation, and the hopes of Sweden were apparently justified by the fact that the mere rumor of an opinion expressed in certain quarters in England that the renewal of the bounty act, which would expire in 1725, was inexpedient, caused the price of Finland tar to rise at once to fourteen shillings per barrel.[3]

---

[1] B. T. Plants. Gen., L: 58.
[2] Memorial of Mr. Godin, Dec. 22, 1724, B. T. Plants. Gen., L: 59.
[3] Ibid.

It is not easy to estimate exactly to what extent influences issuing from government circles affected the decision of the Board of Trade respecting the bounty question, but it seems probable that the deplorable state of the navy finances may have been an important factor in the question of the renewal of the Naval Stores Act. The enormous expenses of the late war had necessarily fallen heavily upon the Navy, and there had been serious charges of maladministration brought against the Navy Board throughout the war. Their debt was made the subject of debate in Parliament in the winter of 1721, and the king, in a speech from the throne, said that this was the "most heavy and burdensome part of the national debt."[1] The fact that navy bills were at high discount may, very likely, have had something to do with the discontent of the merchants who complained that they got little benefit from the premiums. It is even more probable that the state of their accounts strongly influenced the Navy Board themselves in their attitude towards the encouragement of plantation stores.[2]

A certain Mr. Godin, who, at a hearing of the West India merchants before the Board of Trade, proposed that as a means of increasing the navy revenue all ships from the plantations bound for Africa, Europe, etc., be obliged to touch at Great Britain and pay "lights" before returning to America, stated his opinion that the colonists could not object to this regulation, "especially if the bill for the bounty on pitch and tar now ready to expire be renewed."[3] This gentleman seems to have been criticised for favoring the colonies at the expense of England by advocating the continuation of the act; for he was at the pains of writing to the Board an explanation of his position.[4]

---

[1] "Collection of Parliamentary Debates," 1668-1761.

[2] It will be remembered that the accumulation of the national debt was regarded as a very serious matter just at this time, and that the discussion of the bounty on naval stores was coincident with the attempt to provide for the debt through the agency of the South Sea Company.

[3] Memorial from Mr. Godin, B. T. Plants. Gen., L: 59.

[4] Second memorial from Mr. Godin, Jan. 5, 1725, B. T. Plants. Gen., L: 60.

He says that he never did, and never would, pursue the colonies'
interests any further than was consistent with those of Great
Britain; that the real objection to renewing the bounty, which
the Navy offered as most prevailing with the Treasury, was
that the Navy debt was still unprovided for while the bounty
had, since the peace as well as in war, multiplied so fast as to
amount to £50,000 a year.   Some check on this drain of the
public treasure was certainly necessary; but his project of requiring ships to pay "lights" would remedy all that and reduce
the output by more than one-half, without depriving the colonies of the encouragement, or threatening the manufacturing
interests of the mother-country.

In view of the continued protests of the merchants against
the rules,[1] the Navy Board took the various petitions into consideration and suggested the following compromise: After the
removal of the duties, a premium, continuing for ten years, of
(1) £3 per ton on tar from prepared trees ; (2) £1 10s. per ton on
tar made in the common way (to continue for three years only);
(3) £1 per ton on pitch ; (4) 14s. on masts ; (5) the removal of
the duties on rosin and turpentine.   They claimed that the per-
sistence of the merchants in their objections to the rules was
inconceivable; for Mr. Bridger had tried the experiment, and
the tar which he had sent home had been tested and approved
at Woolwich.[2]   But although the Bounty Act expired in this
year, nothing further was done about its renewal until 1729.
when, by 2 Geo. II., c. 35, Sect. 3, the premiums were continued
on the old method, but at a reduced scale : tar, per ton, £2 4s.;
pitch, per ton, £1 ; turpentine, per ton, £1 8s.

Section 2 provided that, "Whereas the inhabitants of the
plantations not being experienced in the prescribed methods of

---

[1]Memorial from merchants trading to the plantations, B. T. Plants.
Gen., L: 44.   Petition of importers and dealers, L: 54.   Certificate
of good quality of American tar, L: 55.   Proof received from one Mr.
Carey that it is impossible to make tar from green pines, L: 56.
Protest of Bristol merchants against the rules, L: 63.   These mer-
chants sent in a fresh petition in 1725.

[2]Report of the Navy on the merchants' petition, Plants. Gen , L: 61.

making tar, cannot yet furnish any great quantities according to 8 Geo. I. c. 12, as a further encouragement any tar made according to the rules shall be entitled to £4 per ton."[1]

The encouragement of the importation of hemp, from which so much had been expected, had thus far proved insufficient. This was one of the most expensive commodities which the government purchased from the East Country, the price in war having sometimes risen to 27 shillings or more per hundred weight. Joshua Gee stated, in 1721, that it was impossible to carry on the navigation of England without a supply of seven or eight thousand tons of hemp from abroad; and that the Czar, with his usual penetration, would doubtless engross that product and set his own prices, so that it was worth while to offer extraordinary inducements to the American plantations.[2] From all accounts of the soil of the several plantations in America, it had been thought perfectly possible to raise a sufficient supply for the navy from thence, if cultivation could be sufficiently encouraged. So great stress was laid upon the advantages of raising hemp in America that the premiums offered were greater than those for other species of stores. Still, although the governors wrote of the fitness of the soil in their provinces and the interest of the people to try for the bounty, and although every one of the schemes for colonization included plans for raising hemp, none was imported for sixteen years after the passing of 3 and 4 Anne, c. 9.[3] There are several reasons which account for this failure. In the first place, hemp requires an exceedingly rich soil,[4] and while the plant adapts itself to a considerable variety of climate, it is exceedingly sensitive to frost. Although it might be grown to a certain extent in New England, the climate and soil of Maryland and Carolina were better adapted to

---

[1] These bounties were continued to 1764 by 16 Geo. II. c. 26, Sect. 2; 24 Geo. II. c. 35, Sect. 11, and 31 Geo. II. c. 25, Sect. 3.

[2] Memorial from Joshua Gee, B. T. Plants. Gen., L: 24.

[3] Cf. table, Appendix B.

[4] "In Missouri the term 'hemp land' is deemed a compliment to the fertility of the soil thus designated." Patton, "Natural Resources of the United States," p. 407.

the best quality of product than those of any of the other colonies.[1] Aside from the requirements of soil and climate, hemp requires great care in planting, gathering and preparing for market ; and, even with the printed rules sent over for their guidance, the people had not practical skill needed to bring the cultivation of the plant to perfection. Even if they had possessed the skill, there was scarcely any seed in the country, and the planters were too poor to buy. The surveyors and the governors suggested that the government should send over enough of the best Riga seed to set the people on the cultivation of a product which would be very profitable, if once brought to perfection.[2]   A good deal of seed was distributed, but, as Joshua Gee pointed out, there was great risk in sending seed by a long water journey, unless it was properly packed. "Some, indeed," he said, "have carried over several parcels in order to sow it, but their unskillfulness in the nature of seeds made their trial and experiments unsuccessful, for they shipped it off and put it in the hold, where it heated, which rendered it altogether useless; for seed is a thing of that tenderness that if once heated and afterwards sown, it will not grow."[3] Another discouragement, according to Thomas Coram, was the fact that the premium went to the importer, and not to the planters who took the risks and expended time without getting any particular benefit.

Attempts were made in several provinces to provide more direct encouragement for the producers by bounties granted by the local assemblies, and, during the period of the great depreciation of the currency, by allowing hemp to pass as money. Massachusetts, New Hampshire and Connecticut granted bounties, and Maryland allowed hemp to be received in part

---

[1] At the present time the great hemp producing states are Kentucky and Missouri.

[2] Letter from Mr. Bridger to the Board of Trade, New Eng., W: 69, and letter from Lieut. Gov. Wentworth, X: 68, Report of Board of Trade to Privy Council, B. T. Entry Bk. L., June 12, 1735.

[3] Gee's Memorial, B. T. Plants. Gen., L: 24.

payment for debts.[1] Massachusetts, in 1735, passed an act allowing the payment of taxes in hemp for two years.[2] Other suggestions were made elsewhere, such as the payment of quit-rents in hemp or tar;[3] but in spite of these strenuous efforts by the home government and the local assemblies, the importation of hemp did not increase perceptibly. According to accounts sent to the Board of Trade from the custom house, only 316 hundred weight was brought in between 1712 and 1729.[4] Nevertheless, the government persisted in their efforts. In 1731, the drawback on the re-export of foreign unwrought hemp to the plantations was disallowed,[5] as an indirect encouragement to the American product. The old bounty on hemp expired in 1741, but after a term of years a new bounty was offered on hemp and undressed flax, to continue for 21 years:[6] £8 per ton for the first 7 years ; £6 per ton for the second 7 years ; £4 per ton for the third 7 years.[7]

Macpherson, who gives statistics of the exportation of naval stores from Carolina, where alone hemp seemed to thrive, for a considerable number of years, mentions no hemp until the year 1769, in which 290,095 pounds were sent over. I find no mention of exportation from any other colony ; so that even these later extraordinary encouragements which the government offered for this commodity, at the time when, as Adam Smith put it, " England was alternately courting and quarreling with the colonies,"[8] failed to produce the desired results.

To sum up the history of the bounty legislation on naval stores, the attempts of the government to stimulate the produc-

---

[1] B. T. Md. Docts., H: 22, D; "Acts of Massachusetts Bay," April, 1731, Ch. XVI; B. T. New Eng., W: 64, X: 29; B. T. Proprieties S: 52.
[2] Felt, "History of the Massachusetts Currency," p. 92.
[3] Memorandum in B. T., North Carolina, B: 14.
[4] Reports from the Custom House, B. T. Plants. Gen., P: 14.
[5] 4 Geo. II, c. 28, Sect. 7.
[6] January, 1764-1785, 4 Geo. III, c. 26.
[7] By 26 Geo. III, c. 53, passed in 1760; this bounty continued for 21 years.
[8] "Wealth of Nations" Vol. II, p. 229.

tion and importation of products which the American plantations could furnish in return for British manufactures covered a period of three-quarters of a century, beginning with the reign of Queen Anne and continuing until the war of the Revolution interrupted the commercial relations between the colonies and the mother-country. The three groups of naval stores on which bounties were offered were (1) tar and allied products; (2) hemp; (3) masts and timber. From the mercantilist point of view, the legislation affecting the first group may be regarded as, on the whole, successful in stimulating importation; that affecting the second group, as an almost complete failure. The history of the trade in timber differs in one important particular from that in other species of stores, in that the former involved something more than the mere exploitation of natural products which could be exported with little or no expenditure of capital, whether money or skilled labor, in the improvement of the soil or of methods; while trees were a natural product which merely required the simple processes of felling and sawing to prepare them for the market. The circumstances which were destined to determine the success or failure of the encouragement of masts and timber were of an entirely different character, in most respects, from those which affected tar, pitch and hemp; they will, therefore, be treated separately, in a subsequent chapter.

CHAPTER II.

The Preservation of the Woods.

One of the most important results of the commission sent to
New England on behalf of the project for stimulating the importation of colonial stores[1] was the creation of the office of
Surveyor General of the Woods in America. It is not quite
accurate, perhaps, to say that the office was created at that time,
for there had been a surveyor of the woods in New England for
half a century. Edward Randolph, of sinister reputation in New
England as the enemy of charter-government, on being made
Surveyor General of Customs in America in 1691,[2] had petitioned for the office of Surveyor of the Woods in addition, saying, as proof of his experience, that he had been made surveyor
of woods and timber in Maine in the year 1656, where he had
marked and registered many large trees; and he "did provide
and deliver to his Majesty's stores forty masts and bowsprits
of largest dimensions, and in great measure restrained the inhabitants from waste." Apparently his request was granted, but
neither he nor Jahleel Brenton, who subsequently combined
these two offices, accomplished much for the preservation
of the timber. Governor Bellomont complained to the Lords
of Trade of Brenton's neglect,[3] and recommended that the office of surveyor be combined with the collectorship of customs
for New Hampshire, at a salary of £50. This was the amount
paid to Randolph and Brenton, who, wrote Bellomont, "never
did a sixpence of work." Brenton had remained in England
and employed one Ichabod Plaisted as deputy surveyor, who
being interested in some saw-mills, was of as little use as his

---

[1] See Part I, Ch. I, pp. 9-14.
[2] Petition of Edw. Randolph, B. T. Plants. Gen., A: 15.
[3] Bellomont to the Board of Trade, B. T. New Eng., F: 17.

superior.   While in New England, Bridger had complained of Brenton's neglect, and so had Wallis, one of the contractors who furnished masts for the Navy.[1]   The charge received further confirmation from the fact that both Massachusetts[2] and New Hampshire,[3] in trying to maintain their innocence of the waste which had been reported to the Board of Trade as constantly practiced in those provinces, insisted that no complaints had ever been heard from Brenton or his deputy.   The accused surveyor stoutly defended his reputation, and informed the Board that Wallis had accused him because he wanted the post for himself.[4]

However this may have been, the office was of little importance until Mr. Bridger, in 1705, recommended to the Board of Trade that, "to further the importation of stores in accordance with the act of Parliament just passed,[5] some fitting person be appointed Surveyor General of the Woods."[6]   The Board of Trade had become so impressed with the disastrous consequences of the waste of the woods which was constantly reported to them from all quarters, notably from Governor Bellomont and from the New England commissioners, that they had taken steps to procure an act of Parliament for the stricter preservation of the "King's woods."   The charter of Massachusetts granted by William and Mary had specified the size of trees which were to be reserved for the king, but it was thought that too much latitude was given by the charter; and, furthermore, while by ancient custom the reservation of trees for the royal navy had been understood to hold for New Hampshire as well as Massachusetts, there was no express

---

[1] Bridger to the Board of Trade, B. T. New Eng., F: 20, and communications from Wallis enclosed in a letter from the Earl of Jersey to the Board.

[2] Memorial from Massachusetts Bay Colony to the King, B. T. New Eng., K: 16.

[3] Memorial from New Hampshire, B. T. New Eng., K: 53.

[4] Brenton to the Board of Trade, B. T. New Eng., N: 33.

[5] 3 and 4 Anne, Ch. 9.   See p. 63.

[6] Memorial from Bridger, B. T. Plants. Gen., H: 4.

law to that effect. The Board accordingly suggested that Governor Bellomont might fitly be directed to urge the respective assemblies to pass acts for the more effectual regulation of the woods; or, if unable to accomplish this, that he should send over headings for a bill to be passed by Parliament. Such a request was sent to Lord Bellomont in January, 1701; but the governor's death occurring shortly after this, no definite action was taken with regard to the prevention of waste until 1705, when the Naval Stores Bounty Act was passed.[1] The fourth clause of the act forbade the cutting of "any pitch pines or tar trees within any of the New England colonies or New York or New Jersey, not being within any fence or actual enclosure, under the growth of 12 inches in diameter at three foot from the earth, on the penalty or forfeiture of £5 for each offense." This regulation, it will be noted, merely provided for the small pitch pines used for making tar. It was to be the chief duty of the new surveyor to see that the provisions of this clause were strictly carried out. In view of the encouragement to the production of pitch and tar offered by the act, he was further required to teach the people the proper methods of preparing these commodities.

Mr. Bridger proposed himself for the office, as a person fitted for those duties by his late experiences as commissioner in New England, and in March, 1705, he formally petitioned the Queen for the post.[2] His proposition received further support from a petition made to the Board of Trade by certain merchants and traders to New England, who, after the publication of the new act, requested that a person well skilled in the production of naval stores should be sent over to instruct the people.[3] The Board of Trade, on the 14th of November, 1705, recommended to the Queen that Mr. Bridger be made surveyor of the woods, at a salary not exceeding £200 sterling per an-

[1] 3 and 4 Anne, c. 9, Sect. 4.
[2] Memorial from Bridger and petition to the Queen. B. T. Plants. Gen., H: 4 and 6.
[3] Petition from merchants and traders, B. T. New Eng., P: 35.

num.[1] This recommendation being approved, the Board were
directed to prepare a commission and draw up instructions for
Mr. Bridger.[2] The instructions are interesting as showing
how the conception of the office had enlarged.[3] The surveyor
was to show to the several governors in New England his commission and such part of his instructions as might be necessary
from time to time; to survey the woods in New England and
do all he could for their preservation; to restrain the people
from taking liberties with the king's woods; to instruct the
people in the best methods of making pitch and tar, and in the
choice of trees, and of land proper for hemp; to correct mis-
takes and to see that the pitch and tar shipped were free from
dross, and that each cask was properly labeled with the name
and address of the maker. He was further directed to urge
governors to get acts passed for the promotion of the undertaking, and for the prevention of abuses; and when he had
done all this for New England, to do the same in other colonies.
Lastly, he was required to keep a strict account of all proceedings, and to report progress to the Secretary of State, the Board
of Trade, and the several governors.

In February, 1706, Bridger received his formal commission.[4]
Having been heralded by a circular letter to the colonial governors informing them of his appointment and directing them
to support and assist him in every possible way,[5] the surveyor
arrived in Boston, September 15th, and soon afterward proceeded to Piscataqua. From here he wrote to the Board of
Trade that he had found the woods in a bad state, and that the
survey was very difficult on account of the Indians. He would

---

[1]Recommendation from the Board of Trade, B. T. New Eng.,
P: 35.
[2]Direction to the Board to prepare instructions, B. T. Plants. Gen.,
H: 24.
[3]Copy of instructions for Mr. Bridger, B. T. New Eng., Entry
Bk. F., December 19, 1705.
[4]Copy of Mr. Bridger's commission, B. T. New Eng., Q: 45.
[5]Circular letter to governors of the plantations, B. T. Plants. Gen.,
Entry Bk. D., February 4, 1706.

like money for a guard, and he needed two deputies for the Piscataqua on which there were seventy saw-mills. He further desired that an order should be sent to the various customs offices to send him a quarterly account of what quantity of each species of stores was annually exported.[1] The task which an officer of this character had before him was not easy, for the distances were great, necessitating much travel by bad roads, or no roads at all, in all kinds of weather. Governor Dudley, in writing to the Lords of Trade, spoke most appreciatively of the discouragements of the undertaking, and expressed his opinion that Mr. Bridger ought to have two or three deputies to the eastward, and at least one in the south, in order to do his duty properly.[2] Bridger himself wrote that he had been obliged to appoint three men to take charge of the loggers at the three great rivers, for although the people seemed greatly inclined to promote the raising of stores, there was still enormous destruction going on by reason of the wasteful methods of the loggers and their illegal encroachments on the king's woods. Later he wrote that he had proper directions for making tar printed, but the people were so fond of their own way that nothing could draw them off. Unless they could see the new method tried before their eyes, they would not consent to take the trouble to go to work properly. The only remedy would seem to be to appoint him to make such a trial or else to incorporate a company to set about the trade heartily.[3]

In the meantime, according to the instructions received from the government, Governor Dudley issued a proclamation calling all persons to the due observance of the charter and to the assistance of the surveyor.[4] Bridger drew up a bill for the preservation of the woods, forbidding anyone but the surveyor or his deputy to mark any trees with the broad arrow, on penalty

[1] Mr. Bridger to the Board of Trade, B. T. New Eng., Q: 52.
[2] Gov. Dudley to the Board of Trade, B. T. New Eng., R: 27.
[3] Mr. Bridger to the Board of Trade, Oct. 24, 1706, B. T. New Eng., Q: 53. This was at the time of the Penn. Co.'s petition for a charter.
[4] Proclamation by Gov. Dudley, issued Dec. 15, 1707, B. T. New Eng., R: 69.

of £5 for every tree so marked. The governor tried to get this act passed in Massachusetts, but, although it went through the Council, it failed to pass the Assembly.[1]

Owing to the nature of his office and, possibly also, to the arbitrary manner in which he defended the "king's prerogative" in the woods, Bridger came to be very much disliked. Mr. Mico had a special grudge against him, and, according to Bridger's story, threatened to turn him out if it cost £10,000.[2] Another of his enemies, John Phillips, charged him with bribery and corruption in selling privileges to the people to cut trees and allowing others to send masts out of the country without a license.[3] To make his position more secure, Bridger suggested to the Board of Trade a plan by which he could serve several ends at once. If he could be made Lieut. Governor of New Hampshire and Captain of Fort Ann, with sixty men, a lieutenant and an ensign, he proposed to set forty men to work in the woods part of the time, at 12 pence per day in addition to their wages as soldiers; by this means he would engage to make from 1,500 to 2,000 barrels of tar a year. The position, moreover, would give him greater authority in his office as surveyor. Under the present circumstances, he complained, his life was threatened, for he was in danger of being shot if he went into the woods.[4]

Bridger had now held his office for ten years, and there was talk of his removal. Fearing that in spite of his protests, the slander of his enemies was gaining credence with the Board of Trade, he returned to England in January, 1715, to counteract the movement against him and petition for the renewal of his commission.[5] Colonel Burgess, who expected to go over to

---

[1] Copy of Act of Massachusetts Bay, B. T. New Eng., S: 10.

[2] Mr. Bridger to the Board of Trade, Feb. 1710, B. T. New Eng., S: 89.

[3] Memorial against Mr. Bridger from John Phillips, B. T. New Eng., Entry Bk. H., Aug. 1, 1710.

[4] Mr. Bridger to the Board of Trade, B. T. New Eng., T: 32.

[5] Memorandum that Bridger's petition for the renewal of his commission has been referred to the Board of Trade, B. T. New Eng., V: 50.

New England as Governor Dudley's successor, brought against the surveyor formal charges of neglect of duty and bribery, offering as evidence written vouchers from Mr. Mico, Benjamin Wentworth, Thomas Coram and others.[1] An investigation of the charges was ordered, but Bridger succeeded in clearing himself to the satisfaction of the Board of Trade.[2] It appears that, aside from the accusations against Bridger, numerous representations had been made from time to time of the uselessness of the office of surveyor now that the French and Indian wars were over; so that the Admiralty had induced the king to issue an order in council (December, 1714), that Mr. Bridger's allowance should be discontinued.[3] Bridger expressed his own views of the importance of the surveyorship,[4] and one Archibald Cummings, who himself aspired to the office, prepared a memorial to the effect that, in his opinion, it was of greater consequence than ever to the public service to keep up the care of the woods, because in peace the inhabitants extended their farms, cut up more timber and made new settlements in the timber regions. He further suggested that the office was not so expensive in peace as in war, and closed his discourse with remarks on Bridger's mismanagement, intimating that he himself was eminently qualified to undertake the office and would be pleased to receive the appointment.[5] The first part of this memorial seems to have made more impression on His Majesty than the last suggestion; for, while it was decided to continue the office, it was Bridger, and not Cummings, that received the appointment.[6]

---

[1] Communications from Col. Burgess, B. T. New Eng., V: 51, 52; deposition of Benj. Wentworth, V: 53; representation of Thos. Coram, shipbuilder, V: 54.

[2] Letter from Mr. Bridger defending himself from the charges made against him, B. T. New Eng., V: 59.

[3] Petition of Mr. Bridger, B. T. New Eng., V: 96.

[4] Communication from Mr. Bridger relative to the requisites of a surveyor, B. T. New Eng., V: 65.

[5] Petition of Archibald Cummings, B. T. New Eng., V: 66.

[6] His Majesty orders the Board to continue Bridger in his office and prepare his commission, B. T. New Eng., V: 83.

On arriving in New England, the surveyor found that great destruction had gone on during his absence, and that Lieut. Governor Vaughan had removed three of the deputies and put in creatures of his own, who "suffered anything to be done which pleased the people."[1]   There had been an act passed by Parliament in 1711,[2] for the more effectual preservation of the white pines, of which the best and largest masts were made, and which the loggers cut up for boards in a most reckless fashion. The penalty for cutting "a white or any other pine tree not the property of any private person, such tree being of the growth of 24 inches in diameter or upwards at 12 inches from the earth, "without His Majesty's license," had been fixed at £100 sterling.   For a while the measure may have had some little effect in preventing the ruin of the large mast trees, but Bridger wrote to the Board of Trade soon after his return to the woods, that the people were now spending their energies in cutting up the trees under 24 inches, pleading the act itself in justification; so that unless the act were amended, all the young trees would be ruined.[3]   Another destructive practice of the people was to box one pine tree for turpentine in two or three places at once. The surveyor succeeded in getting an act passed in New Hampshire forbidding the making of more than one box at a time on one tree.[4]   Governor Shute complied with his instructions by issuing a proclamation requiring due observance of the charter and the acts of Parliament passed for the preservation of the woods, and directing all officers to assist the surveyor in seizing trees cut without license and in prosecuting transgressors.[5] Bridger wrote to ask that the then vacant place in the Council be given to him, because it would insure him greater authority and respect.[6]   He seems to have carried with his second com-

[1] Mr. Bridger to the Board of Trade, B. T. New Eng., V: 167.
[2] 9 Anne, c. 22, and B. T. New Eng., Entry Bk. G., Jan. 16, 1710.
[3] Mr. Bridger to Secretary Burchett, B. T. New Eng., V: 130.
[4] Copy of act of New Hampshire to encourage hemp, etc., B. T. New Eng., W: 68.
[5] Copy of proclamation by Gov. Shute, B. T. New Eng., X: 29.
[6] Mr. Bridger to the Board of Trade, B. T. New Eng., V: 167.

mission fresh zeal for the king's prerogative and a determination that no future charges of inactivity should be justified. As the disputes about the ambiguous clause in the charter relating to the royal reservation, and about the king's claim to the woods in Maine waxed hotter, this same zeal of the surveyor continually embroiled him with the New Englanders.[1] In fact Jeremiah Dummer, the agent for New England, protested to the Board of Trade that Bridger had gone so far as to forbid anyone to enter the woods or to cut any sort of lumber whether fit for the navy or not.[2] The surveyor had been back in New England only ten months, when he received the unwelcome news that he had been superseded and his commission given to Mr. Burniston, whose salary was to begin June 19, 1718.[3] This had been brought about, according to Bridger himself, by the "malicious insinuations of Mr. Dummer—a false and cunning person." In his defense to the Board of Trade, Bridger wrote: "I am of the opinion that my maintaining the king's title to the woods against the charter and the people has disgusted this great man, and I must fall a victim to his malice. The rumor has spread, and the people threaten me and have begun to cut all before them." The people were continually inventing new ways to circumvent him, and he was of the opinion that a new deputy would have a sorry time of it.[4] Bridger was so hard pushed for money, having received no salary for six months, that he wrote that he would be willing to act as deputy for the new surveyor, rather than starve.[5]

Exactly what were the circumstances of Bridger's removal it is not easy to say, for the Board of Trade immediately recommended to the Treasury that his salary should be paid until his successor arrived, "especially as he had not been superseded for any failure in his duty." They also expressed the hope that

[1] Cf. Part III, Ch. I, p. 110-112.
[2] Jeremiah Dummer to the Board of Trade, B. T. New Eng., V: 169.
[3] Mr. Bridger to the Board of Trade, B. T. New Eng., W: 46; Robt. Armstrong to the Board of Trade, W: 47.
[4] B. T. New, Eng., W: 46.
[5] Mr. Bridger to the Board of Trade, B. T. New Eng., W: 47.

the report that Burniston intended to act by deputy was not true; for if Mr. Bridger, who was allowed to have all the qualifications and appeared to have been very active and diligent, had not hitherto been able to hinder the waste, it was not likely that a stranger would succeed.[1] To Bridger himself the Board of Trade wrote a soothing letter,[2] informing him of their recommendation that his salary should go on until he was superseded by some one on the spot, and expressing their favorable opinion of his past service and the hope that "they might be able to give him soon a more favorable account of that matter." They desired him to continue to send them information about the woods and any thoughts about making hemp, bar and rough iron, and potashes; also his opinion about the land in Nova Scotia. Bridger replied, with forcible directness, that he would be very glad to give the information their Lordships desired, but there was no living without a salary.[3] The wily Dummer, he wrote, had contrived to intercept the letter from the Board of Trade allowing his salary until the arrival of the deputy, and having informed Burniston of the contents, kept the letter back until the deputy was appointed.[4] The latter, a Mr. Armstrong, had received no instructions, so that Bridger proposed to continue his work as usual.[5] Armstrong was the collector of customs, and, according to Bridger's undoubtedly biased account, he had been bred a clerk in a country store, and did not know an oak from a pine, nor one pine from another;[6] while, as collector, his business was with the sea and not with the woods.   While Bridger was in New York helping Col. Hunter settle the Palatines, Armstrong had applied to Lord Godolphin to recommend him for deputy surveyor, but the latter had refused to do so

---

[1] The Board of Trade to the Treasury, Feb. 6, 1719, B. T. New Eng., W: 48.

[2] The Board of Trade to Mr. Bridger, B. T. New Eng., Entry Bk. I, Feb. 20, 1719.

[3] Mr. Bridger to the Board of Trade, B. T. New Eng., W: 64.

[4] Letter to Secretary Popple, June 26, 1719.

[5] Copy of vote of thanks to Mr. Bridger passed by the General Assembly of New Hampshire, B. T. New Eng., W: 65.

[6] Mr. Bridger to the Board of Trade, B. T., New Eng., W: 66.

wihtout Bridger's consent. Bridger stated his objection to such an appointment, at the time, on grounds that then appeared satisfactory.[1]

The Board of Trade adopted a laissez-faire policy in regard to the affairs of the woods during the year 1720, neither sending instructions to Armstrong nor recalling Bridger. The latter continued his warfare against the loggers, but although he repeatedly wrote to have his seizures confirmed, he received no word from the Board of Trade for fifteen months and no salary for two years.[2] Meanwhile the loggers, seeing that Bridger received no recognition from the government, defied his authority more boldly than ever, until his position became most embarrassing. "'Tis very hard," he wrote, pathetically, in the twenty-fifth year of his service in the woods, "to serve my King all my life, and to at last want Bread and do the Duty."[3] Toward the end of the year 1720, Armstrong appeared and began his duties, and Mr. Bridger returned to England with testimonials from Governor Shute and Lieut.-Governor Wentworth, praising his industry, skill and honesty, and a certificate from the Council of New Hampshire that the General Assembly had passed a vote of thanks to him for promoting two acts to encourage the raising of hemp.[4] Wentworth showed a special friendliness to him and wrote to the Board of Trade that the reports against him were utterly false.[5] In May, 1722, Bridger made a last effort to induce the Board of Trade to restore him to his office, pleading the increasing need of vigilance now that all kinds of timber had been freed from duty,[6] and the people would be thereby encouraged to destroy the king's woods; and urging the incompetency and lack of experience of Armstrong.[7]

---

[1] Mr. Bridger to the Board of Trade, B. T. New Eng., W: 69.
[2] Mr. Bridger to the Board of Trade, B. T. New Eng., X: 74, 75.
[3] Mr. Bridger to the Board of Trade, B. T. New Eng., W: 104.
[4] Mr. Bridger to the Board of Trade, B. T. New Eng., X: 77.
[5] Lieut.-Gov. Wentworth to the Board of Trade, B. T. New Eng., X: 71.
[6] 8 Geo. I, c. 12, passed 1722.
[7] Mr. Bridger to the Board of Trade, B. T. Plants. Gen., L: 27.

But this time he pleaded in vain and the under-bred collector of customs continued to hold the place.

Armstrong was no more successful in preventing the destruction of timber than Bridger had been, and he continually wrote home in the old complaining strain of his predecessor.[1] It is scarcely surprising to learn that he was as unpopular as Bridger. Accusations soon began to be sent to the Board of Trade,—accusations of neglect, of disaffection to the government, of oppression of honest traders by extorting heavy sums for clearance, of illegal trading on his own account, and even of perjury. The memorialists, who were traders to New England, insisted that they could prove their charges beyond the shadow of doubt.[2] It was now Armstrong's turn to be dismissed and recalled to England to answer the accusations which had been brought against him.[3] Again Governor Shute, Wentworth and the Council took the part of the surveyor, and he so far succeeded in clearing his reputation that in 1725 he was allowed to return to America and resume his office and his complaints of the physical hardships of his position and the "barbarous treatment His Majesty's officers meet in America that do their duty."[4] In 1728, David Dunbar was made surveyor in Burniston's place, but Armstrong continued to act as deputy.[5] Armstrong wrote to the Lords of Trade describing the difficulties of the office, and suggesting that any supernumerary carpenters and laborers, who could be spared, also a "chirurgeon for accidents," would greatly contribute to reduce the

---

[1] Robt. Armstrong to Board of Trade, B. T. New Eng., W: 102. Robt. Armstrong to Mr. Burniston, B. T. New Eng., X: 29. Robt. Armstrong to Board of Trade, B. T. New Eng., X: 47 and 93.

[2] Memorials from three traders, B. T. New Eng., X: 92 and 95. Certificates and further accusations relating to Armstrong's illegal procedure, B. T. New Eng., X: 96, 98, 99.

[3] In 1723. Memorandum that Armstrong has sailed for England, etc., B. T. New Eng., Y: 20.

[4] Mr. Burniston writes to the Board, about Armstrong's character B. T. New Eng., Y: 22. Armstrong vindicates himself from charges, Jan. 1725, B. T. New Eng., Y: 31.

[5] Order in Council, June, 1728, B. T. Plants. Gen., L: 100.

expense of hiring labor in New England.[1] In June, 1728, an order was passed in council that the surveyor of the woods should reside in one of the plantations and be allowed two or more salaried deputies, one of whom was to be a ship carpenter.[2] The new incumbent was directed to instruct the inhabitants in the culture of hemp and to lose no time in setting apart a royal reservation in Nova Scotia.[3] Dunbar was prevented by illness from sailing for New England on the appointed date, but he sent his brother to superintend the deputies, Armstrong and Slade, who were marking trees in New Hampshire and Maine.[4] Jeremiah Dunbar and the deputies wrote continually of the evils of waste, the impossibility of securing judgments in favor of the king in the prosecutions for illegal cutting, and of the difficulty of securing the masts after they had been seized in the king's name.[5]

Dunbar was displaced in 1744 by Benning Wentworth, son of the late lieutenant-governor.[6] Wentworth got the post of governor of New Hampshire, and that of surveyor-general at the same time, through the personal influence of Tomlinson, the agent for New Hampshire. It is said that the second appointment was assisted by the offer of a consideration of £2,000 sterling to Dunbar.[7] If this is true, it would seem that the office was considered to be lucrative. The strenuous but ineffectual efforts of William Vaughan to obtain the posts of collector of customs and the surveyor of the woods, as being "the most beneficial in the province (Massachusetts Bay) except the governorship,"[8] point to the same conclusion. But as the salary was neither munificent nor, as a rule, paid without urgent solicita-

---

[1] Mr. Dunbar to the Board of Trade, B. T. Plants. Gen., L: 84.

[2] Order in Council, B. T. Plants. Gen., L: 100.

[3] Ibid.

[4] Mr. Dunbar to the Board of Trade, B. T. New Eng., Z: 36, and Mr. Dunbar to Temple Stanyan, America and West Indies, I: 146.

[5] Letters to Mr. Dunbar from one of his deputies, B. T. New Eng., Z: 46, 49.

[6] N. H. Records of Council, p. 12.

[7] Palfrey, "History of New England," Vol. V, p. 180.

[8] Palfrey, "History of New England," Vol. V, p. 183, n.

tion, it is natural to infer that some of the charges brought against the surveyors of ekeing out their income by means not strictly scrupulous, may not have been without foundation.[1] The evidence on both sides is of so uncertain a character that it must be taken with caution and it is not easy to learn the truth. There could certainly have been few inducements other than those of a pecuniary nature to attract aspirants to the office. If the surveyor followed his instructions conscientiously, he antagonized the people, who, resenting the abridgement of their liberties, heaped reproaches on the king's officer and did their worst to make the performance of his duties disagreeable. On the other hand, to accuse the surveyors of lacking tact is to reproach them for not possessing a qualification which time and circumstances rendered exceedingly rare. Even the Board of Trade, who were not remarkable for leniency or consideration in dealing with officials under their superintendence, admitted that although Bridger might not have done his work perfectly, there was much to be said in his defense.[2] When we follow in detail the long struggle of New England lumbermen against the attempt of the Crown to reserve the pick of the mast trees for the royal navy, the difficulties of the surveyor's office will become more apparent.

---

[1] Belknap in his "History of New Hampshire," Ch. XVI, says that Dunbar had £200 salary, and perquisites amounting to £100 which were divided between him and his deputies.

[2] Bridger stated that while he was surveyor, he and his deputies marked 3,030 trees. He, himself, traveled 161 days on account of prosecutions, for which he received no pay. He supported from four to six deputies for nine years at his own charge, and a guard of six for an average of thirty-six days every winter. B. T. New Eng., Entry Bk. H., Feb. 1716.

PART III.

CHAPTER I.

THE GROWTH OF THE LUMBER TRADE IN NEW ENGLAND.

It was unfortunate for the promoters of the policy of utilizing the forests of America for the supply of the royal navy that the chief mast-producing district was New England. They could scarcely have found a more difficult field for exploitation, partly because of what Evelyn called the "touchy humour" of those colonies, and partly because of certain economic conditions which made it by no means easy to divert into English markets their only available staples for foreign export.

Josiah Child, in a pamphlet published in 1692, stated that New England was the most prejudicial plantation to the kingdom, and proceeded to a somewhat elaborate demonstration of his proposition.[1] New England, he said, differed in several particulars from the other plantations. In the first place, the other colonies produced commodities different from those of the mother country, while New England sold fish, lumber and provisions to the West Indies, in return for merchandise which could be re-exported to Great Britain to pay for manufactures, thus diminishing the vent of those necessaries which England would otherwise have supplied to the islands. In the next place, by virtue of their original charters, the New Englanders were not so firmly attached to the mother-country as the other colonies, and their growing political and economic independence ran counter to the theory that the most useful colonies are those that are most dependent upon the central government, and whose trade is made most subservient to the commercial interest of the mother-country. The author was bound to admit that the export of British manufactures to New England was very important, and he could not refrain from complimenting

[1] "Discourse of Trade," 1692, Ch. 10.

the industry and enterprise which was indicated by the extensive commerce of the people with foreign nations and with the French West India plantations. And yet it was claimed that they might be made far more useful to the kingdom by a stricter control of their trade.

The chief industries of New England, on which the people depended for products to exchange for articles they could not produce, and for money to pay for British manufactures, were the fisheries, ship-building and the lumber trade. Lumber was not only an important and profitable article of export, but it ministered directly to the other two industries, and was, in its various forms, in steady demand for domestic purposes. Scarcely any natural product is convertible into so many forms of merchandise, with so little waste, as a tree; while unwrought timber, in the form of masts, bowsprits, and specially-shaped pieces for ship-building, commands high prices ; so that the demand for lumber is bound to be fairly constant. Almost from the beginning, the masts and ship timber of New England found a ready market in foreign countries. To the island plantations, which did not produce timber extensively, were exported materials for house-building, and even frame houses and ready built ships. Cargoes of masts and yards were sent to Guinea and Madagascar in return for slaves. The wine islands exchanged their products for pipe staves; the sugar islands, for barrel and hogshead staves. Before 1650, the trade in these commodities was so heavy that it was feared that the supplies of timber at Piscataqua would fail.[1] The fact that, in 1660, one-third of a saw-mill sold for £250, shows how important the industry was esteemed.[2]

The first saw-mill in America is said to have been set up on the Salmon Falls River, New Hampshire, in 1663,[3] many years before one appeared in England. Once established, the mills multiplied rapidly along the rivers where the water-power could

[1]Weeden, " Social and Economic History of New Eng.," page 200,
[2]Ibid.
[3]Bolles, "Industrial History of the United States," p. 499.

be utilized. When Mr. Bridger went to New Hampshire to enter upon his duties as surveyor, he wrote home that there were over seventy saw-mills on the Piscataqua.[1] Daniel Neal, who wrote in 1720, speaking of the advantages of the Piscataqua and its branches, says: "This is the principal place of trade for masts of any of the king's dominion. Three or four vessels go hence yearly, for the use of the royal navy. Here are ninety saws carried by water-power, and one hundred and thirty teams of oxen constantly employed in drawing logs of timber to the saws." He estimated that, at that time, upwards of six million feet of timber was cut annually, most of which was transported to Boston and the West Indies.[2] The supply seemed so inexhaustible that the cutters in their haste recklessly and promiscuously destroyed the largest trees for making clapboards, shingles and pipe staves. Even the agent of one of the contractors for the royal navy admitted that he saved only one in four. In 1712, Falmouth (Portland) became the chief port of export for masts, instead of Piscataqua (Portsmouth), and this change of center marked an important step in the progress of the timber industry, while the removal of duties on lumber, in 1722, greatly increased the export, especially of heavy unwrought timber. Fleets of vessels of 400 tons, built for the exclusive transport of masts, sailed from Falmouth every year; so that, in order to satisfy the demand for heavy timber, the woodsmen began to cut along the Connecticut River in Massachusetts and Connecticut, as well as in New Hampshire.[3]

Coincident with the rapid increase of the lumber trade was, of course, the growth of ship-building. "Of all the American plantations," said Josiah Child, "His Majesty hath none so apt for the building of shipping as New England, nor none comparably so qualified for the breeding of seamen, not only by reason of the natural industry of that people, but principally by

---

[1] Mr. Bridger to the Board of Trade, B. T. New Eng., Q: 53.
[2] "History of New England," Chapter on "The Present State of New England."
[3] Weeden, p. 578.

reason of their cod and mackerel fisheries; and in my poor opinion, there is nothing more prejudicial, and in prospect more dangerous, to any mother kingdom, than the increase of shiping in their colonies, plantations or provinces."[1]   From the launching of Winthrop's "Blessing of the Bay," in 1631, the industry increased on the Massachusetts coast, under the patronage of the Assembly, which granted special privileges to shipbuilders and provided for the inspection of vessels.[2]   Johnson, in his "Wonder-Working Providence," said, in 1647, that the building of ships was going on gallantly.[3]   In 1676, Randolph mentions, as the centers of this industry in Massachusetts, Boston, Charlestown, Salem, Ipswich, Salisbury, and Piscatauqua; and he enumerates the ships of the province, with their tonnage, as follows: Thirty vessels of 100-250 tons, two hundred of 50-100 tons, two hundred of 30-50 tons, and three hundred of 6-10 tons.   Most of these were fishing ketches, but with the increase in the exports of masts, lumber and bulky goods, and the growing demands of the carrying trade, the tonnage also increased. Toward the end of the century, ship-building was extended to other towns and pushed further inland, where the abundance of timber and the cheapness of living reduced the cost ;[4] and during the first quarter of the next century the industry advanced steadily in New England.   By 1721, Massachusetts launched annually from 140 to 160 vessels.[5]

In 1724, the master builders of the Thames sent in a formal complaint to the Board of Trade that, on account of the great number of vessels built, and likely to be built, in New England, their trade was very much decayed; so that many able shipwrights in their employ had been obliged for want of work to migrate to America and other foreign parts. This loss of skilled labor was regarded as a serious prejudice not only to the ship-builders, but also to the nation, in case of the necessity,

---

[1] "Discourse of Trade," Ch. 10.
[2] Weeden, p. 156.
[3] Weeden, p. 207.
[4] Weeden, pp. 253, 254.
[5] Weeden, p. 579.

in some extraordinary emergency, of fitting out the royal navy.[1]
Mr. West, the "King's Council," delivered as his legal opinion
on the above memorial, that as the law then stood, complaint
against American shipping would be no more justifiable than
complaint against the building of ships at Bristol.[2] The incident shows how clearly the great importance of this industry
was recognized on the other side of the water, and how little
(except, perhaps, during the period of depreciated currency)
New England felt the need of the forced development of a new
industry, like the manufacture of pitch and tar or the cultivation
of hemp.

Recalling the history of the Naval Stores Act of 1705,[3] it becomes apparent why the enthusiasm of the New England merchants cooled so suddenly, when the advantages of the promised
bounty appeared doubtful. The tar which they exported was
chiefly the product of Carolina, bought by way of exchange,
and they felt no great interest in the encouragement of that industry in New England. Owing to the inadvertent neglect of
these colonies and the lax administration of the navigation laws,
the New Englanders were making great strides in trade with
other continental plantations, with the West Indies, and with
foreign countries. Their energies were concentrated upon the
industries which were rapidly advancing their material pros-
perity. It was, therefore, to be expected that whatever interfered with their independent trade would meet with vigorous
and unremitting opposition. So far as timber was concerned,
it would seem to have been a comparatively simple matter to
force New England masts, yards and bowsprits into the English market by restrictive legislation, or to coax them in by
bounty acts. But two causes interfered with the engrossment
of these commodities by the mother-country. One was the
success of the New Englanders in evading the navigation laws;
the second was the attempt of the government to insist upon the

---

[1] Petition of master ship-builders of the Thames, B. T. New Eng.,
Y: 27.
[2] Opinion of Mr. West, the King's counsel, B. T. New Eng., Y: 28.
[3] Cf. Part II, Ch. I.

reservation of large districts of the best pine and oak woods for the use of the Crown, basing the king's right to such woods on a legal technicality of the charter of 1691.

Timber had not been included among the "enumerated commodities" subjected to duties and confined to the British market by the navigation laws of 1660, because the product was not supposed to be worth controlling. Bridger and Holland,[1] however, wrote home from New England, in December, 1699: "We have discovered a trade to Portugal from this place, in timber, knees, etc., there being no law or act of the country which forbids it."[2] The next year, Governor Bellomont found Mr. Partridge, who was a member of the commission sent to New England and a lumber merchant, engaged in a very lucrative trade with Portugal. Bellomont attempted to prevent the sailing of one of Partridge's vessels laden with timber, and the two became involved in a serious quarrel.[3] Bellomont informed the Board of Trade that Partridge had openly boasted of a profitable voyage his ship had made, by which, for an outlay of less than £300, he had cleared £1,600 at Lisbon. "He has set all the country agogg," wrote the indignant governor, "so that some merchants at Salem are now loading a ship with 12,000 feet of the noblest ship plank that ever was seen in America, and scarce a knot in them. Your Lordships may see by this what vigilance is necessary for a governor of these plantations, and what eternal trouble I am at in contending for the interest of England with the people of my three governments."[4] Partridge and the other merchants protested that the timber sent to Spain and Portugal was not fit for the royal navy,[5] and the Board of Trade sent orders that their ships should be allowed to pass. By the act of 1705, however, the three chief sorts of timber,

---

[1] Holland took the place of Furzer, the Commissioner who died at Barbadoes, Cf. p. 10.

[2] Mr. Bridger to the Board of Trade, B. T. New Eng., F: 33.

[3] Lord Bellomont to the Board of Trade, B. T. New Eng., G: 21, 41. Lord Bellomont to Mr. Partridge, Ibid, G: 41.

[4] Lord Bellomont to the Board of Trade, B. T. New York, L: 23.

[5] Mr. Partridge to the Board of Trade, B. T. New Eng., I: 1.

masts, yards and bowsprits, were put on the same footing as the enumerated commodities. But the trade in other kinds of timber and probably by evasion, in masts and bowsprits as well, continued to increase, in spite of occasional protests against the bad policy of allowing countries, which were, or might at any moment become, the enemies of Great Britain, to be supplied by the American plantations. Information was received by the Board of Trade from a sailor of Falmouth, lately come from Calez (Cadiz?) in a Dutch ship, that before he left, there came a fleet of five ships from New England full of stores of masts, oak timber and planks, for that king's service. The informant hoped the matter "would be inquired into and those wicked men punished."

The legitimate export of lumber was surprisingly great. The statistics of the quantities of timber sent from New Hampshire to Lisbon and Cadiz between 1712 and 1718 speak for themselves:[1] 2,176 pieces of oak timber from 30 to 55 feet long, 98,-925 oak planks, 3,035 oak joists, 43,880 pine planks, 22,000 pine boards, 93,250 pipe staves, 42,360 hogshead staves, 5,470 oak bolts, 168 standards, 12 knees, 1,511 spars, 8 bowsprits, 135 stocks, 1,100 ash rafters, 173 pine timbers (?), 152 carriage trucks.

Occasional complaints continued to be made of this trade of New England with Spain and Portugal, especially because it contributed to the destruction to the king's woods. In 1729, the Board of Trade were informed through Dunbar's deputy in New Hampshire, that there were in that place seven ships laden with planks for Spain. "'Tis very moving," he says, "to hear complaints at home for want of timber, when His Majesty's subjects here are supplying his enemies abroad."[2] Nevertheless, although the Crown officers in New England laid so much stress upon the prevalence of this foreign trade, the home government showed a general indifference to the consequences.

---

[1] Wm. Cornes to the Board of Trade, Dec. 15, 1718, B. T. New Eng., W: 63.
[2] Letter from Mr. Slade to Mr. Dunbar, B. T. New Eng., Z: 46.

The Treasury, it is true, recommended to the Board of Trade, in 1727, that they should procure an act of Parliament to prevent the exportation of masts and timber from the plantations to foreign ports; but nothing came of their proposal, and although an act relating to plantation timber was passed two years later, no provision was made for any such restriction. As late as 1739, Benning Wentworth, of Piscatauqua, had large contracts with an agent at the court of Spain for oak timber,[1] and it was not until 1765 that the blow was struck at illicit foreign trade, by the prohibition of export to any but English ports. In 1766, non-enumerated articles were placed under the same restrictions as enumerated commodities.[2]

Let us now turn to that more serious disturbing element in the commercial relations between New England and the Crown, which has been alluded to as the effort to maintain the king's prerogative in the woods. The charter of Massachusetts Bay, granted in 1691, distinctly reserved to the Crown all trees 24 inches in diameter upwards of 12 inches from the ground, growing upon any tract of land not hitherto granted to any private person; and all persons were forbidden to cut or destroy such trees, without a license from the Crown.[3]   At the granting of the charter, it had not yet been decided to make any attempt to rely exclusively on the royal woods in America for the masting of the fleets; but there were one or two contractors employed to fetch over a certain number of masts yearly, and it was to these con-

---

[1] Weeden, p. 578.
[2] 6 Geo. III.
[3] Poore's "Charters," Part I.   The clause reads: "And lastly for the better providing and furnishing of Masts for our Royal Navy, Wee doe hereby reserve to Us all trees of 24 inches in diameter upwards of 12 inches from the ground growing upon any soyle or Tract of Land within Our said Province or Territory not heretofore granted to any private persons. And Wee doe restraine and forbid all persons whatsoever from felling, cutting or destroying any such Trees without the Royall Lycence of Us, Our Heires and Successors; for every Such Tree soe felled, cutt or destroyed without such Lycence had or obteyned in that behalfe, anything in these presents conteyned to the contrary in any wise Notwithstanding."

tractors that the license referred to in the charter was intended
to be given. Very little attention seems to have been paid by
the inhabitants to this clause of the charter, and when the government undertook the systematic protection of the woods, it
was made a part of the surveyor's business to see that the king's
rights were maintained. The governors were also instructed
to secure obedience to the charter.

When Mr. Bridger began his duties, he found that it was by
no means an easy matter to distinguish the king's land from
private grants. He wrote home that thousands of acres were
held without any claim whatever.[1] The bounds had never been
accurately surveyed, and there was the utmost confusion of
titles. Bridger proceeded to stir up trouble, by accusing the
navy contractors or their agents of cutting without license and
of exceeding their contracts. The accusations were made
hastily, and in such a manner as to bitterly antagonize the
agents. It appears that John Plaisted, factor for John Taylor,[2]
was ordering his men to cut trees, from the largest down to 20
inches in diameter, in spite of the governor's proclamation to
respect the charter. Bridger ordered the men to stop, and
obliged Plaisted to give £2,000 bonds not to cut any more.
Plaisted insisted that the charter was no law, and the more
Bridger opposed him, the more he cut. Finally, be produced
a license from Queen Mary, dated 1691, and said that he could
cut as long as the contract was not fulfilled. Bridger declared
that he had cut a very great number of masts above his contract, but Plaisted pleaded that he had cut none except on his
own grounds or within townships.[3] Upon the question whether
the expression "grants to private persons" was intended to include townships, hung the long controversy which raged between surveyor and inhabitants. Bridger wrote to the Board
of Trade that, hitherto, he had preserved trees in the townships,
taking the meaning of private grant to be single persons, not

[1] Mr. Dunbar to the Board of Trade, B. T. New Eng., R: 29.
[2] Cf. Part I, Ch. I, p. 6.
[3] Mr. Bridger to the Board of Trade, B. T. New Eng., R: 39.

towns; and such grants to be improved estates, or enclosed lands. The townships were very indefinite, and sometimes twenty miles long and not one-tenth inhabited.[1] If the Queen were to be excluded from these, it would render the masting more difficult and expensive, because the masts must be cut far up in the woods, miles from the water side, where there was danger from the Indians, and whence the trees could be hauled only when there was snow on the ground.[2]

Bridger got into a violent quarrel with another contractor, Collins, and his agent, Mico, by seizing 300 masts which, the latter claimed, had been legally cut.[3] Mico tried to get Bridger put out of office,[4] and, according to Bridger's story, at the same time offered him money to keep still about his misdeeds. Bridger wrote to the Board of Trade that Mico had been guilty of the following offenses: He and his workmen had every year cut the full number of masts, and delivered only three shiploads; they had exceeded the number and dimensions of the contract; "last year, in particular," he says, "they destroyed near 30 masts 29 to 36 inches in diameter, which I saw, and measured some." There were nine ship-loadings due, or 576 masts, which should have been delivered yearly, according to the contract, and their not having been sent was "a great disappointment to the service." All the masts were rotting in the

[1] Mr. Bridger to the Board of Trade, B. T. New Eng., R: 39.
[2] Mr. Bridger to the Board of Trade, B. T. New Eng., S: 89. Burnaby, in his "Travels Through the Middle Settlements of America," (1759–60), thus describes the process of hauling trees: "They never cut them down but in times of deep snow, as it would be impossible, in any other season, to get them down the river. When the trees are fallen, they yoke from seventy to eighty pair of oxen and drag them along the snow. It is exceedingly difficult to put them first in motion, which they call "raising" them; and when they have once effected this, they never stop on any account whatsoever, till they arrive at the water's side. Frequently some of the oxen are taken ill, upon which they immediately cut them out of the gear, and are sometimes obliged, as I was told, to destroy five or six pair of them."
[3] Mr. Bridger to the Board of Trade, B. T. New Eng., S: 97.
[4] Cf. Part II, Ch. II, p. 92.

rivers of Piscatauqua, which was a damage to Her Majesty of more than £17,000, at £30 a mast. Moreover, Mico's workmen had let other loggers into Her Majesty's woods where they had cut many hundred masts.[1]

Governor Dudley tried to smooth matters over, not knowing which side to support.[2] The Board of Trade encouraged Bridger to maintain the charter and to prosecute offenders, and at the same time they sent to Solicitor General Eyre for his interpretation of the clause in the charter, especially of the words "private persons."[3] The legal authority conceived the phrase to mean particular persons, not towns, bodies politic, etc. But he submitted his opinion that the Crown had no more right to cut timber on lands granted to bodies politic than on those granted to private persons; for when the inheritance of the lands was granted, by virtue of former charters where trees were not reserved, trees passed as part of the inheritance, and a reservation by a subsequent charter could not deprive the proprietors of interest in those trees. Therefore, the clause did not hold in regard to any trees growing on lands granted by former charters, but only to those on lands granted under that of 1691. This interpretation, coming from the counsel of the Crown, savors of loose construction, and, as a decision, it is not very clear. The Assembly of Massachusetts insisted that they had it in their power to grant all lands and woods without the townships, or give them away, as they pleased; and that they could lay out new towns, which they proceeded to do, to the distraction of the surveyors, and in spite of the expostulations of the governor. Bridger wrote, in despair, that if such practices were sanctioned, the king would soon be unable to have a mast without buying it of the proprietors. What else the people

---

[1] Deposition against Mico by Bridger, B. T. America and West Indies, I: 8s.

[2] Gov. Dudley to the Board of Trade, B. T. New Eng., Entry Bk. G., April, 1710.

[3] Secretary Popple (of the Board of Trade) to Solicitor General Eyre, B. T. New Eng., S: 93.

might take it into their heads to do, he was at a loss to imagine, as they had just appointed a committee of the Upper and Lower House, to sit on the king's title to the woods, which would remain undetermined till the next session![1] In the meantime, although urged to continue the prosecution of transgressors, Bridger received no confirmation of his seizure of Collins's masts, although he wrote again and again for instructions. This failure of the government to support the Crown officers in their duty, or to give them sufficient authority to act without waiting for specific orders, interfered very seriously with the efforts of the surveyors to defend the king's interests.[2] However tactful he might be, one royal officer was not a match for the entire population, who took sides with the loggers, or for the courts, where judge and jury alike were offenders.[3] Even the lieutenant-governors of New Hampshire were, in most cases, New Englanders interested in the lumber business. Bellomont had complained that the appointment of Partridge was like setting a wolf to keep sheep, for he was a millwright, and the interest of England was "neither in his head nor heart."[4] Vaughan, who became lieutenant-governor in 1715, was not a millwright, but he was concerned in several saw-mills which had occasioned great destruction of the woods.[5] The plea was urged on all sides that the charter was of no account, so far as the king's right to the woods was concerned. But for other purposes, according to Bridger, "it was like the law of Medes and Persians." If this charter, "the Magog and Idol of these people," were

---

[1] Mr. Bridger's letter to the Board of Trade, July 14, 1718, in B. T. New Eng., Bundle V.

[2] Letter from Mr. Armstrong to the Board of Trade, complaining of the lack of support on the part of the government, B. T. New Eng., W: 74.

[3] Mr. Bridger to the Board of Trade, B. T. New Eng., Entry Bk. G., May 22, 1711, and B. T. America and West Indies No. 1, fol. 20.

[4] Letter to Secretary Stanhope relating to Col. Vaughan's appointment as Lieutenant-Governor of New Hampshire, B. T. New Eng., V: 70.

[5] Ibid.

taken away, he wrote wrathfully, "His Majesty's prerogative would shine bright."[1]

The "levelling people" of Massachusetts now began to assert an even bolder claim against the king. During the years 1718 and 1719, the settlement of Maine had begun to increase rapidly. This province contained even finer mast trees than New Hampshire, and since the laying out of new towns meant the erection of new saw-mills, Bridger, as surveyor, protested against what he deemed a flagrant offense against the rights of the Crown. The champion of the Massachusetts Assembly was Elisha Cooke, whom the governor had put out of the Council,[2] but who had continued to be returned to the legislature from Boston. Cooke attacked Bridger with great insolence, asserting that the king had no sort of right to the woods in Maine, for that province had been a private grant to Sir Ferdinand Gorges, with no reservation of woods. The heirs of Gorges had granted it to Mr. Usher, of Boston, who sold it to Massachusetts for £1,250.[3] Bridger contended that the charter gave Massachusetts no right whatever to purchase Maine; at that rate, they might buy up Rhode Island or Connecticut, if they chose.

When this new phase of hostility was reported to the Board of Trade, they at once sought legal counsel on the subject.[4] Mr. West, His Majesty's counsel, submitted his opinion that there was no license to purchase lands granted, by express words, in the charter of Charles I.; but, in any case, since that patent had been reversed in chancery, in 1684, by a judgment upon a *scire facias*, the province had thereby reverted to the Crown. Therefore, the inhabitants could have no claim to Maine, except by some new title which had accrued to them since their incorporation by William and Mary,—which was

[1] Mr. Bridger to the Board of Trade, B. T. New Eng., Entry Bk. G, May 22, 1711.
[2] Letter from Mr. Bridger to the Board of Trade, July 14, 1718.
[3] Ibid.
[4] Record that the Board had sent Mr. Bridger's letter of July 14, and other papers to Mr. West, B. T. New Eng., Entry Bk. I, Oct. 7, 1718.

impossible, there being no license in their last charter to purchase lands. King William had evidently considered Maine and Massachusetts as one province, and it was impossible that one part of a province could be the private property of another.[1] It was certainly the part of a conservative legal adviser to the Crown, like Mr. West, in a question of authority to give the king the benefit of the doubt; and according to the letter of the law he could hardly have decided otherwise. On the other hand, it is needless to say that, had the New England colonies contented themselves with the powers to which a literal interpretation of the wording of the charter of 1629 entitled them, they could scarcely have attained the state of virtual autonomy of which the champions of the king's prerogative complained. But by 1719, it was too late to undo the work of nearly a century. Cooke undoubtedly represented an extreme view of the extent of authority which Massachusetts possessed, either by charter right or by usurpation. Whether the right of purchase was recognized or not, Maine, as a part of Massachusetts, was still under royal jurisdiction, and the king must have had as much right to the woods in Maine as he had to those in Massachusetts: in other words, so far as the right of reservation held for Massachusetts, it held for Maine.

The act of 1711[2] had enumerated all the New England provinces, as subject to a reservation of the trees of specified dimensions. But in view of the acrimonious temper of the Massachusetts Assembly, and the disposition of the inhabitants to resent the interference of the king's officers with the exercise of their most lucrative industry, it is not surprising that they should have upheld Cooke as the defender of their rights. Therefore Cooke continued unhindered to buy up the timber lands of Maine and offer them for sale. He even offered Bridger's deputy a lot, at a low price. On Bridger's advice, the deputy refused to buy; but, said Bridger, "anybody else may buy it, and what is to become of the king's masts?"[3] Cooke

---

[1] Mr. West's report on the above papers, B. T. New Eng., W: 22.
[2] 9 Anne, c. 22.
[3] Mr. Bridger to the Board of Trade, B. T. New Eng., X: 72.

proceeded to buy up two old grants made under the government of New England, in 1641 and 1671, but never taken up; one grant contained 800 acres, the other 500, and Cooke laid them out in Maine outside of the townships, in the very best part of the timber land.[1] The boldness of Cooke encouraged the lumbermen, who cut wherever they liked, especially destroying the young trees under 24 inches in diameter, pleading the act of 1711.[2] They were further encouraged in their evil ways by the failure of the home government to confirm the seizures which the surveyors had made, or to send them any instructions as to the disposal of the prizes.[3] It will be remembered that this was the period of the inter-regnum in the woods, when Bridger had been displaced and the new surveyor had failed to send any deputy—a state of affairs which seems to have been regarded by the loggers as a special providence, of which they were not slow to take advantage. Bridger wrote: "It was easier for one man to preserve the woods five years ago, than it would be for five men now." He reported that over 120 trees were cut without license, by Taylor's agent, during the winter of 1720.[4] Taylor's contract called for two ship-loads only, but the agent had agreed with the lumbermen to cut enough to load six ships, without giving the surveyor any notice.[5] In the summer of that year, Bridger wrote to the Board of Trade that he had lost several prosecutions, because it was impossible to prove that the trees had been cut on unappropriated lands. The *onus probandi* rested with the king, and all the witnesses were against him and "never knew anything about anything."[6] Governor Shute also complained to the Board of Trade that the "main drift of the House" was to persuade the people that the king had no right to the woods.[7] Armstrong,

---

[1] Mr. Bridger to the Board of Trade, B. T. New Eng., X: 30.
[2] Mr. Bridger to Secretary Burchett, B. T. New Eng., V: 130.
[3] Mr. Armstrong to the Board of Trade, B. T. New Eng., W: 74.
[4] Mr. Bridger to the Board of Trade, B. T. New Eng., W: 104.
[5] Mr. Bridger to the Board of Trade, B. T. New Eng., X: 79.
[6] Ibid.
[7] Report from Gov. Shute to the Board of Trade, B. T. New Eng., X: 36.

Bridger's successor, further informed the Board, in 1721, that he had found in New Hampshire upwards of 25,000 logs cut, two-thirds of them being from 24 to 30 inches in diameter, and 20 feet long. They had been brought to the saw-mills to be sawn into planks. He believed that, where one mast was sent home, five hundred were cut or destroyed;[1] and that owing to the unfortunate wording of the act of Parliament,[2] ("not being the property of any private persons") the evasion of the law by the laying out of townships, was increasing; which, he said, was a practice that ought to be prohibited. He enclosed a list of the exports of New Hampshire for the year 1718-19, to show how injurious the lumber trade was to the interests of the kingdom.[3] This list included:

912,331 boards.	78,450 pipe staves.
1,014 oak planks.	654 pine planks.
615,050 shingles.	518 spars.
199 masts.	43 yards.
171 bowsprits.	485 oak timbers.
60,072 joists.	23,905 oar rafters.
63,950 barrel staves.	171,660 hogshead staves.
5,515 (ft.) square timber.	73 knees.
171 anchor stocks.	26,910 (ft.) oak planks.
32,141 (ft.) best pine plank.	11,000 clapboards.

In 1722, the act was passed which removed the duty from timber.[4] The fifth clause dealt with the preservation of white pine trees, in view of the fact that the laws already made for those trees had been found insufficient. Apparently, it was not thought possible to insist that a township was not to be regarded as a private person, for the clause read: "No white pine not growing within any township shall be cut, felled or destroyed without His Majesty's license first had or obtained." A graduated scale of penalties was attached, according to the

---

[1] Mr. Armstrong to the Board of Trade, B. T. New Eng., X: 47.
[2] 9 Anne, c. 22.
[3] Mr. Armstrong to the Board of Trade, B. T. New Eng., X: 47.
[4] 8 Geo. I, c. 12.

size of the tree destroyed, and the burden of proof whether the
tree had been cut within or- without the township was made to
lie with the owner.

The removal of duties from timber and lumber was intended
to attract importation to England, but, as Bridger pointed out,
it certainly offered a temptation to the lumbermen to poach on
the king's preserves; and, as experience proved, it encouraged
the formation of new townships in the pine-growing regions.
Deputy Armstrong, in his report of September 1, 1724,[1] stated
that there were many good trees outside the townships, but
these were, for the most part, difficult to reach and to transport,
and that the government of New Hampshire had within the last
five or six years, and especially since the last act of Parliament,
granted four or five townships, each ten miles square, where the
best timber grew, without even sending home to have their
grants confirmed by the king, as they had been accustomed to
do in times past. There were within the towns, he said, vast
tracts belonging to the Crown, which the inhabitants claimed
only by right of possession, and which might be recovered, if
the Crown would examine into the original grants. The
Board of Trade wrote to the Treasury that something must be
done by Parliament, since the people insisted on their own interpretation of the township clause.[2]

The Council stated, in their instructions to David Dunbar,
who was made surveyor in 1728, that nothing in that act was to
be construed to take away the right reserved to the Crown, by
the charter of William and Mary, to trees *less* than 24 inches
in diameter, whether within or without townships.[3] But Slade,
one of the deputy surveyors, wrote that unless there were an act
forbidding the cutting of any white pines whatever, in or out of
the towns, there would be few masts left in the province.[4] Arm-

---

[1] Report from Mr. Armstrong, B. T. New Eng., Y: 24.
[2] The Board of Trade to the Treasury, B. T. New Eng., Entry
Bk. I, Feb. 6, 1726.
[3] Order in Council, June 13, 1728, B. T. Plants. Gen. L: 100.
[4] Jeremiah Dunbar to David Dunbar, B. T. America and West
Indies 1: 146.

strong had recently seized 200 logs which the people had tossed into the rivers and floated down to the mills.[1] This was one of the wiles by which the loggers sought to outwit the surveyors and make it impossible to prove where the trees had been cut.

When Armstrong offered the condemned trees for sale on the king's account, no one appeared to buy them, so that the expense of the condemnation fell on the Crown.[2] The history of this seizure illustrates the spirit which prevailed on both sides. No sooner was the deputy's back turned, than the "country fellows" cut up forty of the finest of the condemned trees and carried them off. This so exasperated the surveyor that he went to all their saw-mills (more than one hundred) and seized 1,300 logs, some of which were forty inches in diameter, beside 280 white pines not yet cut up into logs. Dunbar also seized 94 logs in Berwick. He reported that scarcely any trees were left standing, within six or seven miles of the waterside, between Boston and Kennebec.[3] "I have showed the people the directions for making hemp, pitch and tar," he wrote, "but while they can cut pine trees and steal them, they don't think it worth while to do anything else, and are inclined to laugh at us for proposing it."[4]

Matters were becoming daily more serious, and the Board of Trade felt that drastic measures were imperatively necessary, and they wrote to the Treasury to that effect. The Treasury replied that if remedy could not be had, save by a new law, the Board might prepare a draft for such an act.[5] A bill was, accordingly, drawn up, which, with some slight modification, passed in April, 1729.[6] The act stated that, whereas, since the passing of 8 Geo. I., c. 12, great tracts of land, where trees fit

---

[1] Deputy Slade to David Dunbar, B. T. America and West Indies I: 147.
[2] Deputy Slade to David Dunbar, B. T. New Eng., Z: 49.
[3] Jeremiah Dunbar to David Dunbar, B. T. New Eng., Z: 51.
[4] Ibid.
[5] Treasury to the Board of Trade, B. T., New Eng., Y: 73.
[6] 2 Geo. II, c. 35.

for masting grew, had been erected into townships, in order to evade the provisions of the said act, it was enacted that after September 29, 1729, no person or persons within Nova Scotia, New Hampshire, the Province of Maine, Massachusetts Bay, Rhode Island, Providence Plantations, Narragansett County or King's Province, and Connecticut, in New England, or New York and New Jersey in America, or any other provinces, should cut, fell or destroy any white pine trees, except such as were the property of private persons, "notwithstanding the said trees do grow within the limits of any townships laid out, or to be laid out hereafter in any of the said colonies," without license from the Crown. It was further enacted (Section II.) that "no person within the province of Massachusetts Bay should presume to cut or destroy any white pine 24 inches or upwards, 12 inches from the ground, not growing within some soil or tract of land the said province granted to some private person before October 7, 1690, without His Majesty's license, on penalty of forfeiture according to 8 Geo. I., c. 12." Here then, at last, we have the ambiguous clause of the charter made clear and the status of the township defined.

In December, 1729, Colonel Dunbar wrote home that the publication of the new act was having a good effect on the loggers, who had since applied to him, in great numbers, to know if they might cut trees of any dimensions, because everything was included in the act, without exception.[1] But even an act of Parliament was not sufficient to prevent abuses entirely, for what could not be done legally, was accomplished by evasion and connivance.

The impossibility of obtaining judgment in the king's favor, in the prosecutions, shows more than anything else the determination of the people to nullify the claim of the Crown, in defiance of the king's officers and of Parliament. There is an interesting letter from Colonel Dunbar, written in February, 1730, which describes the methods of justice pursued in New Hampshire.[2] It appears that a certain man was convicted for

---

[1] Col. Dunbar to the Board of Trade, B. T. New Eng., Z: 91.
[2] Col. Dunbar to the Board of Trade, B. T. America and West Indies, No. 1, fol. 183.

cutting a 36-inch tree, and fined £50 sterling. One-half of the fine, according to the act, went to the informer. Dunbar said that it was reported that this informer had agreed to divide the sum with the convicted person, who was to have the whole made good to him by his confederates, for not having informed on them for cutting 75 large trees, in the same place. On another occasion, a "king's witness" with a citation in his pocket was arrested for debt at the door of the court, and the king's officer obliged to pay the debt, "lest other witnesses should be terrified from appearing." Upon the breaking up of the court, several were heard to say, that, if they must not cut trees, they would girdle them, and then the king might take them. Girdling meant cutting off a strip of bark three or four inches wide, quite around the tree, to prevent the sap from rising, which would destroy the tree or make it fit only for boards. Another practice in which the people indulged was to deliberately cut down the trees marked with the broad arrow, and "in derision of the king's officers" put a similar mark on trees of other timber and of no value. A very vexatious inconvenience arose from the fact that the Piscatauqua separated New Hampshire from Maine, which was under the jurisdiction of Massachusetts; so that offenders prosecuted on the Maine side had to go to Boston, along with witnesses and the surveyor, a distance of 140 miles, in the severe winter weather, to be tried by a "poor, superannuated gentleman, near eighty years old, who already distinguished himself very partial to the country."[1]

Prosecutions under these circumstances were practically useless. Dunbar suggested that it would be greatly to His Majesty's service if George Jaffrey, the Deputy Admiral for New Hampshire, who was "of good understanding and always respectful of His Majesty's instructions and zealous in his interest," might be permitted to hold court on the other side of the river, for the purpose of trying the seizure cases. A short time after the writing of this letter, the surveyor seized some masts which had been cut in Maine. He sent to the Advocate Gen-

---

[1] Judge Byfield.

eral, to get permission for Jaffrey to hold court on the Maine side. But to oppose the king's interest, according to Dunbar, Governor Belcher prevailed upon the old judge to depute another man, who had always appeared in opposition to the king.[1] In 1732, Dunbar wrote again, that he was completely discouraged by the behavior of the Admiralty. The loggers scorned the king's officers; offenders were tried by friends equally guilty; and Judge Byfield himself was interested in Cooke's saw-mills.[2] Colonel Westbrook, the undertaker for masting the navy, was carrying on a large lumber trade. Everywhere, private interest was set before the king's service. "English acts require English hearts and hands to execute them," wrote the surveyor.[3] There were, probably, two sides to this, as to most stories, and it looks as if the behavior of even English officials frequently left something to be desired. Belknap, in his "History of New Hampshire,"[4] says that Dunbar, who had been a colonel in the British service, used to go to the saw-mills, seize and mark great quantities of lumber, with the air and manner to which he had been accustomed in his military capacity. He abused and threatened the people, and then wrote to the Board of Trade about the impertinence of the loggers and their threats against his life. "That class of men," says Belknap, "are not easily intimidated, and he was not a match for them in that species of controversy which they have denominated 'swamp law.'"

One incident, which happened about the year 1736, is described by Dunbar himself to the Board of Trade as a riot at Exeter in which an attempt was made upon his life. He complains bitterly of the indifference of Governor Belcher, who was his enemy, toward the affair.[5] The circumstances are described by Belknap as follows.[6] Dunbar sent his men to seize some lum-

[1] Col. Dunbar to the Board of Trade, B. T. New Eng., Z: 222.
[2] Col. Dunbar to the Board of Trade, B. T. Letters, Aug. 25, 1732.
[3] Ibid.
[4] Belknap, "History of New Hampshire," Ch. XVI.
[5] Memorial from David Dunbar, B. T. Plants. Gen., N: 26.
[6] Belknap, "History of New Hampshire," Ch. XVI.

ber at Exeter. While they were regaling themselves at a public
house and boasting what they intended to do next day, a number of persons, disguised as Indians, attacked and beat them;
others cut the rigging and sails of their boat and made a hole in
the bottom. The discomfited party fled to the boat and made
off, but, of course, began to sink. They regained the shore
with difficulty and hid till morning, when they returned on foot
to Portsmouth. Dunbar, to avenge this insult, summoned the
Council, to whom he described the riotous proceedings at Exeter as a "conspiracy against his life by some evil-minded person, who had hired Indians to destroy him." He requested the
governor to issue a proclamation commanding all magistrates
to assist in the discovery of the rioters. Somehow the rumor
got abroad that the governor's pretense to favor the surveyor
was deceitful, and that the rioters were the governor's best
friends; so that, by a well-managed delay in issuing the proclamation, the culprits escaped. Belknap thinks that Belcher did
all he could, but that the disguise of the men was so complete
and their understanding with one another so good that no proof
could be obtained. It is further related that Dunbar went to
Dover to seize some boards belonging to one Paul Gerrish.
Dunbar threatened with death the first man who should obstruct his intention ; Gerrish retorted with a similar threat
against the first man who should remove his boards. The surveyor's prudence appears to have got the better of his courage,
for he retired without further parley.[1] In 1759, one of the deputies of Benning Wentworth, who was then surveyor, complained to the Board of Trade that he had been "thrown into
the water with intent to kill," by Dan and Seth Whitmore, in
the execution of his office, and unlawfully imprisoned by William Pipkins.[2] From this it is evident that the struggle between the surveyors and the lumbermen went on unabated.

Whether the government persisted in their efforts to enforce
the acts of Parliament, during the next fifteen years, I am un-

[1] Belknap, "History of New Hampshire," Ch. XVI.
[2] "Petition of Daniel Blake, late Deputy Surveyor," B. T. Plants.
Gen., P: 10.

able to say; nor is it possible to determine to what extent the
irritation of the New England woodsmen may have laid the
foundation for the resentment which culminated in 1776. At
all events, the facts presented in this chapter furnished clear
evidence that, so far as one branch of industry is concerned,
the economic independence of New England was declared and
maintained many years before the final rupture with Great
Britain.

CHAPTER II.

The Rise of Manufactures.

The systematic suppression of all attempts of the colonists to manufacture woolens, linen, iron tools and utensils, or anything else which would otherwise be bought directly from Great Britain was a part of the colonial policy which has already been described. It was entirely natural that England should have found it most advantageous to work up the raw materials of the British Isles and the American plantations into manufactured articles for foreign export. It was equally desirable, from the government point of view, that foreign nations should not be allowed to buy directly from the plantations raw materials or food supplies which England could control ; and that they should not supply manufactured articles to British colonies.

Here the national economists ran on the horns of a dilemma. The British colonists in America were, at the outset, essentially an agricultural people. Had they been a primitive people, they might have been economically self-sufficing, since the variety of soil and climate favored the production of enough to supply the necessities of life, when once inter-colonial barter should be established. But, being civilized European settlers accustomed to luxuries of dress and a high standard of living, they desired many articles which they could not, for many generations, have brought to perfection by their own industry. If the balance of their trade with the mother-country had been perfectly adjusted, they could still, in a clumsy fashion, have exchanged food products and raw materials for manufactures, without much distress for lack of the precious metals as a medium of exchange. But, as a matter of fact, if they bought more than they sold, which they in every way were encouraged to do, they were expected, somehow, to procure coin to pay for the balance.

One of two courses was open to the colonists : either to send their goods to the markets of the West Indies or of Europe, where they could sell for cash, and, at least in case of the Dutch, buy manufactures cheaper than in England ;[1] and so, by circuitous and skilfully managed voyages, obtain gold and silver to export to Great Britain in payment for what they bought there ; or they must give up foreign luxuries and, by simplifying their tastes and style of living, content themselves with homespun linen and woolen clothing, and home-made tools and implements. Either of these courses was sure to meet the disapproval of the home government.

What happened in England was the inauguration of a contradictory system of legislation, by which, on the one hand, inter-colonial and foreign trade was more and more closely restricted and manufactures discouraged; while, on the other hand, the colonists were offered a compensation for the loss of foreign markets, by the encouragement of the staples already established in some of the colonies, or by the attempted creation of new staples in the less fortunate provinces, like New England. The need of the government for cheaper naval stores had seemed to statesmen to offer a key for the solution of the problem. If, they reasoned, we can successfully stimulate the importation of stores from those colonies that are suited to produce them, and which, at the same time, lack returns for the manufactures they buy of us, we shall materially benefit the plantations and by the same means free ourselves from dependence on the northern crowns, which now supply us with those commodities and drain us of our gold and silver.

What happened in the colonies, was a continuous struggle to make both ends meet. So far as they were permitted, they obtained bullion by a wonderfully involved process of trade with the West Indies, and with Spain, Portugal and France. When the thumb-screws of restriction were applied, they smuggled or otherwise evaded the law. Even so, their gold and sil-

---

[1] Bolles, "Industrial History of the U. S.," Chapter on "Manufactures."Hutchinson, " History of Massachusetts Bay," Vol. II, p. 438.

ver was steadily exported to Great Britain, until there was very little left ; then they were forced to manufacture for themselves.

The "Letter to a Member of Parliament," written in 1720,[1] exactly describes the situation: "Their (the New Englanders') delight is to wear English manufactures, but the difficulty of coming at them is very great. They have no silver mines—nothing to send but pitch, tar, turpentine and ships, which would go but a little way toward clothing such a number of people. Therefore they are forced to visit the Spanish coast and pick up traffic, and to carry lumber and provisions to the sugar plantations and to the logwood cutters at Campeachy, exchanging for the products of those islands, which they generally send to England ; they are forced to catch fish and make pipe and barrel staves to send to Portugal, Spain and the Streights ; and, lastly, to build great numbers of ships which they sell, with the cargoes, in Portugal, Spain and Europe. Thus they make a shift to scrape up about £150,000 per annum, to pay for the goods they buy of us. It is almost incredible that they raise so much. As it is, they are forced to fall on woolen, linen, iron and leather manufactures."

Let us see to what extent these manufactures were actually carried on. In 1640, owing to the scarcity of money, the General Court of Massachusetts "took into serious consideration the absolute necessity for the raising of the manufacture of linen cloth, etc." They ordered that the magistrates and deputies of the towns inquire what seed there was in every town, what men and women were skillful in breaking, spinning and weaving, and what means there were for providing wheels ; to devise courses to raise materials, and to teach boys and girls to spin. They were also to take into consideration the spinning and weaving of cotton wool.[2] On October 7th, of that year, the Court ordered that, " for the incouragement of the manufacture of linen, woolen and cotton clothes, whosoever shall

---

[1] Cf. Part II, Ch. I, p. 56.
[2] Mass. Records, Vol. I, p. 294.

make any sort of the clothes fit for use and shall shewe the same
to the next magistrate or to two of the deputies of this Court,
upon certificate thereof to this Court or the Court of Assistants,
the party shall have allowance of three pence in the shilling of
the worth of such cloth according to the value certified."[1] This
bounty was to continue for three years. We hear of the allowance having been given to Goodman Null and four others, for
83¼ yards of cloth valued at 12 pence per yard, but the measure
was repealed the same month (June, 1641), as being too great a
burden. Fifteen years later, very definite action was taken to
encourage home manufacture, by setting women, girls and boys
to spinning. The officials were required to assess every family
for spinners, every one so assessed to spin for thirty weeks each
year one pound per week of "lining, cotton or wooling, and
so proportionably, for halfe or quarter spinners, under the penalty of twelve pence for every pound short." Spinning classes
began to be formed in the town.[2] About 1643, some twenty
families from Yorkshire, trained in the cloth manufacture, settled at Rowley, Mass., and set up a fulling-mill ; so that Rowley surpassed all the other towns in the making of homespun.
Imported wool was chiefly used at this time.[3] The number of
fulling-mills increased considerably toward the end of the
century.

Along other lines, also, signs of industrial activity were not
wanting. Smelting, forging and refining of iron were going
on in Lynn down to 1683, and there were iron works started at
Braintree.[4] In 1646, Joseph Jenkins got a patent for 14 years
to build a mill for making scythes ; and he invented " divers
other engines for making divers sorts of edge tools."[5] The
leather trade was active, and the wearing of leather by men and
women was one of the results of the poverty of the country people.[6] Shoes were made in Boston and New Haven, but the

[1] Mass. Records, Vol. I, p. 454.
[2] Weeden, p. 196.
[3] Weeden, p. 177.
[4] Ibid.
[5] Weeden, p. 182.
[6] Bolles, Chapter on " Manufactures."

industry did not begin to flourish till the middle of the eighteenth century.[1] Household utensils, especially pewter dishes, were manufactured generally ;[2] and the hat trade was sufficiently vigorous to call forth an act of Parliament for its suppression.[3]

It is impossible, here, to enumerate all the industries which sprang up in the colonies or to go into the details of the progress of each branch. Probably the government heard very little about many of the minor manufactures, but they were continually informed of the growing danger of the colonies running into the woolen manufacture. The spinning and weaving of wool and flax were the objects of the special jealousy of Parliament, which feared competition with the great national industry, if the colonists should begin to export their own manufactures. Even if they made merely enough for their own use, the decrease in the exportation of English goods to the plantations would be a serious misfortunte. Consequently, the act of the Virginia Legislature, in 1684, to encourage textile manufacture was promptly annulled ; and in accordance with the same policy, an act of Parliament was passed prohibiting the export of wool from one plantation to another.[4]

William Penn himself, in his " Proposals for the Benefit of Trade,"[5] wished to forbid the provinces to obstruct the passage of ships carrying English goods from one plantation to another by imposing customs ; " for it plainly incommodates and discourages the king's subjects and puts them upon shifting for themselves without the need of such goods, and so far prevents the consumption of our English growth and manufactures, and hurts, thereby, trade and navigation."

The Board of Trade, at the outset, took the matter of the woolen industry in America into consideration, along with the proposals for importing naval stores. Almost without excep-

---

[1] Weeden, p. 184.
[2] Weeden, p. 308.
[3] 5 Geo. II, c. 22.
[4] 10 and 11 William III, c. 10, Sect. 19.
[5] B. T. New Eng., A: 60, I.

tion, the petitioners for privileges pleaded the certain increase of colonial manufactures, unless the minds of the people could be diverted by the raising of naval stores. The Board began to make definite inquiries about the extent of sheep-raising and the wool trade. Brenton, the surveyor of customs in New England, reported, in 1704, that the chief sheep-raising districts were Nantucket, Martha's Vineyard and some small islands in the bay ; also, Rhode Island, Block Island, and Canonicut in Narragansett Bay. The reason that wool growing was confined to the islands was the prevalence of wolves on the mainland. Some sheep were raised along the sea-border near Boston, but this required the hired labor of shepherds, which was very expensive, so that the towns were mostly supplied by the islands. "Since the wool act," said Brenton, "we have used our endeavor to prevent the carrying of wool from the islands to the main, but I do not think it possible wholly to prevent it, for some of these islands lie very near—within a half or a quarter of a mile of the main. The country is large and the officers so few, that it may be carried in boats and canoes, in the night, from one place to another, notwithstanding all that the officers can do. But the inhabitants cry aloud that this act does not intend to hinder the carrying wool by water from one place to another in the same colony, of which opinion are most of the lawyers here. The act has had the effect that those towns which cannot be supplied but by stealth, nor without great charge and hazard (involved in smuggling) are now endeavoring to raise sheep and keep them by shepherds." Brenton goes on to say that in a recent journey he made it his business to inform himself on the subject, and he found that, in some towns where formerly there were not one hundred sheep kept, there would shortly be a thousand ; and the islands which once supplied the towns were now working up their own wool for wearing apparel, in much greater quantities than formerly, instead of selling their wool for money "wherewith to purchase a finer sort of woolen manufactures from England."[1] This description is

---

[1] Mr. Brenton's account of the condition of New England, B. T., New Eng., N: 33.

an excellent illustration of the effects of restrictive legislation on remote colonies, bent upon their own economic interests. A year or two later, Bridger, the surveyor, informed the Board of Trade of the "dangerous growing manufacture of wool in New England," and the large importation of wool-combs and cards for the purpose, 155 dozen cards having been brought in within three months.[1]

Shortly after the arrival of Bridger's letter, the Board of Trade received a curious proposition from London merchants, which, ridiculous as it was, showed the eagerness of the woolen merchants to ward off the decrease in their trade. Their suggestion was, to force the planters to clothe their white, black and Indian servants, or slaves, in coarse woolen clothes of English manufacture, purchased by barter of commodities, such as naval stores, "which," they said, "is no more than the Dutch, French and Spanish do to their plantations."[2] The Board of Trade answered the petitioners, with unusual sense, that this could not be done, unless the assemblies in the several plantations, or Parliament, agreed to pass acts compelling it. They held that the ware and merchandise ought to be recommended by goodness and cheapness, rather than forced on them by law, "which is the greatest discouragement to trade." "Obtaining such laws," they observed, "seems to meet with general opposition. The petitioners would better apply themselves to encouraging trade by sending over samples of linsey woolsey, etc. The people have been induced, by proper encouragement, to desert from manufacturing woolens and apply themselves to pitch and tar."[3] This last statement was a somewhat premature jump at conclusions, inasmuch as the first ship-load of stores, since the passing of the Bounty Act, was only then on the way, with the surveyor's warning that, unless the bounty were allowed on their first essay, the people would immediately return

---

[1] Mr. Bridger to the Board of Trade, B. T. New Eng., Q: 34.

[2] Propositions from Messrs. Bubles, Ashton, Pacey and others, B. T. Plants. Gen., I: 9.

[3] Report of the Board of Trade on the merchants' proposition, B. T. Plants. Gen., Entry Bk., D, Dec. 3, 1706.

to spinning and weaving. The history of the attempt to raise pitch and tar in New England has been related.[1]

In 1708, Bridger wrote of the fulfillment of his prophecy. The people had returned to the woolen manufacture, " so that not one in 40 but wears his own carding and spinning." "When I tell them they can get money by the trade (in tar and pitch) to buy two coats while they are carding and spinning to make one, they will not believe unless they see it tried before their eyes."[2] The next year, he wrote again that the woolen manufacture was constantly increasing, instead of the production of pitch and tar, although it was to be hoped that, when the frontiers were less exposed, conditions would be more favorable to the latter industry.[3]

New York, like the New England provinces, lacked commodities to make returns for English goods, which want, wrote Lord Cornbury to the Board of Trade, " sets men's wits to work, and has put them on a trade which I am sure will hurt England, in a little time, viz., the woolen manufacture on Long Island and Connecticut. These colonies, which are but twigs to the main tree, ought to be kept entirely dependent upon and subservient to England, and that can never be if they are suffered to go on in the notions they have, that, as they are Englishmen, so they may set up the same manufactures here as people may do in England."[4] In 1708, Caleb Heathcote, then a member of the Council in New York and an applicant for a contract to supply naval stores, reported to the Board that three-quarters of the linen and woolen which the people used was made by themselves, and if this were not stopped, they would carry it a great deal farther. Some persons had asked his assistance in setting up a manufactory of fine stuffs, but he had discouraged the design.[5] Governor Dudley, of Massachusetts, reported, in 1709, that the woolen trade with England had

---

[1] Cf. Part II, Ch. I.
[2] Mr. Bridger to the Board of Trade, B. T. New Eng., R: 53.
[3] Mr. Bridger to the Board of Trade, B. T. New Eng., S: 46.
[4] Docts. relating to the History of New York, Vol. IV, p. 1166.
[5] Docts. relating to the History of New York, Vol. V, p. 63.

greatly abated and that the people were clothing themselves with their own wool. This state of affairs he attributed, partly, to the excessive prices of all English goods, which made it impossible for the countrymen to buy them, and, partly, to the fact that the returns for England in payment passed through so few hands, that most people had no share in them and could not get money to pay for imported goods.

The only remedy which Dudley could suggest, was that the government should encourage lumber trade with the colonies, and that Her Majesty should build great ships in New England. Unless something of this sort could be done, the woolen trade would grow less every year, in spite of the increase in population. The people were proud enough, said the governor, to wear the best cloth of England, if chopping, sawing, and building ships would pay for them.[1] The policy suggested by Dudley was much more rational than the attempt to force the people to make pitch and tar, for lumber and ships were the natural staples of New England. Hitherto, for reasons explained in a previous chapter, the importation of lumber had not appeared to the government worth encouragement.[2] The Board of Trade wrote to Dudley, desiring him to do all in his power to prevent the inhabitants from going into woolen or other manufactures, " which, if not timely prevented, might prove very prejudicial to Great Britain."[3] At the same time they laid Dudley's proposals before the Admiralty, with reference to some action for the encouragement of the lumber trade.[4] The act removing the duties was passed in 1722.[5] We have seen how this encour-

---

[1] The Board of Trade, in writing to Gov. Dudley, quote at length a letter from him dated March 1, 1709, B. T. New Eng., Entry Bk. G., Jan. 16, 1709.

[2] Part I, Ch. I, p. 13.

[3] The Board of Trade to Gov. Dudley, B. T. New Eng., Entry Bk. G., Jan. 16, 1710.

[4] The Board of Trade to Secretary Burchett, directing him to lay the matter before the Admiralty, B. T. New Eng., Entry Bk. G., Jan. 5, 1711.

[5] Cf. Part II, Ch. I, p. 77.

agement was hampered by the effort to maintain the Crown's claim to the woods.[1]

In the northern colonies, English clothing was fast becoming a luxury for the well-to-do of the towns. Governor Hunter wrote from New York, in 1715, in answer to inquiries about the extent of the use of homespun, that the people of New York and Albany wore no clothing of their own manufacture, but if their Lordships referred to the planters and poorer sort of country people, the computation had been underrated rather than exaggerated ; although he thought that no homespun was sold in shops. He could offer no remedy other than encouraging industries that would be useful to England ; but, he observed, " a law to oblige those who are not able, to wear English manufactures, would be a law to go naked."[2] In 1719, Mr. Bridger reported so great an increase of the woolen manufacture, that scarcely a countryman came to Boston but clad in his own spinning. Everybody encouraged this and discouraged trade from England, saying that it was a pity any goods were brought over. The importation of cotton wool from the West Indies contributed greatly to home manufacture and ought to be prohibited.[3] There were said to be more than 20,000 sheep on Nantucket, and very many in Rhode Island and Block Island.

A New Englander's point of view appears in a " Discourse on the Trade of New England," written by Mr. Banister, in 1715, in answer to some queries put to him by the Board of Trade.[4]. " The difficulties under which trade labors are," he says, " first, the heavy duties on the products which New England could best supply to Great Britain, namely, masts, planks, boards, etc.; secondly, the importation of New England exceeds the exportation, which, if not balanced, will bring this double

---

[1] Cf. Part III, Ch. I.
[2] Docts. relating to the History of New York. Vol. V, p. 457.
[3] Mr. Bridger to Mr. Popple, B. T. New Eng., W: 65.
[4] B. T. New Eng., B: 91. Mr. Banister was a New England merchant in London, who on July 6, 1715, was called before the Board of Trade and questioned regarding the land bank scheme, naval stores and the preservation of woods and fisheries. He promised to hand in a report in writing, which he did July 15th. This is the discourse referred to in the text.

evil — it will oblige us to set up manufactures of our own, which
will entirely destroy the naval stores trade and employ the very
hands that might be employed on stores. The mischief appears
certain ; the remedy is easy. Since the prices of English goods
became so dear, nine years ago, this put the colonies on making
buttons, stuffs, kerseys, linsey woolsey, shalloons, flannels, etc.,
which has decreased the importation of those provinces above
£50,000 per annum. In those days, they had Spanish gold and
silver and a New England coin to make the balance, of which
they sent home from £30,000 to £70,000, annually, until it was
all gone. The exportation from England has increased actually, but not relatively, for the simple reason that three men
require more clothing than two. The want of money necessarily arises from the difference between our import and export,
obliging us to make the balance in money when we had it ; and
the necessity of the government calling for a paper credit, which
obtained a currency in all payments and purchases and made
way for the easy shipping of all our gold and silver, and the
necessity ceasing with the war, the Treasury sinks all paper,
and leaves us without a medium and in a helpless and deplorable condition.[1] Hence the proposition for a land bank. The
best way to keep the colonies firm to the interest of the kingdom is to keep them dependent on it for all their necessaries,
and not, by any more hardships, to force them to subsist of
themselves. If they once run into manufacturing, what will
they ask from England ? Allow them to keep the balance of
their trade, and they will never think of manufactures. But
if the nature of their trade or great duties on their goods destroy
this balance, they must make for themselves, and will, since
they have plenty of materials; but the notion is wild and un-
grounded of the plantations ever setting up for themselves."

The proposition for a land bank, to which Mr. Banister refers, was contained in a petition signed by 182 gentlemen and
merchants of New England in 1715.[2] In view of the continued

---

[1] For a refutation of this theory of the currency see Wm. Douglass's "Currencies of the British Plantations," edited by Chas. J.
Bullock in Amer. Econ. Assoc. Studies, Vol. II, No. 5.

[2] "Petition of Gentlemen and Merchants for a Land Bank," dated
June 15, 1715. B. T. New Eng., V: 56.

export of gold and silver to Great Britain, and the recall of the
New England bills of credit which had been issued to defray
the expenses of the late war, they desired to establish a bank of
credit on land security. The main purpose of the scheme, as
stated in the petition, was to better enable His Majesty's subjects in New England to cultivate and improve naval stores,
and to take off in greater quantities the manufactures of Great
Britain,—suggestions admirably calculated to prejudice the
Board of Trade in favor of the plan. Nevertheless, the land
bank did not meet with approval.[1]

New England was on the verge of financial ruin. The merchants had drained the province of coin and now complained of
the increasing scarcity of money. The period of inflation covered, roughly, the first half of the eighteenth century. The
following table[2] (of Boston exchanges) will serve to indicate
the rapidity of the depreciation of paper currency, which had
been issued originally to pay for the Canadian expeditions in
the late war, and which continued to be received and held at
par by main force, until it was redeemed in specie paid over to
Massachusetts by Parliament for the ransom of Louisburg.

1702	£133	exchanged for £100	sterling.
1705	135	" " 100	"
1713	150	" " 100	"
1716	175	" " 100	"
1717	225	" " 100	"
1722	270	" " 100	"
1728	340	" " 100	"
1730	380	" " 100	"
1737	500	" " 100	"
1741	550	" " 100	"
1749	1100	" " 100	"

[1] This attempt to establish a land bank resulted in a fierce pamphlet war in Massachusetts. Its failure is attributed to the unpopu-
larity of private banks at this time. A similar scheme was proposed
in 1740. Failing of government support, its originators launched
their project at their own risk; but the bank was declared illegal by
Act of Parliament in 1741. The subject of land banks in Massachusetts has been discussed in detail by Andrew McFarland Davis in
the "Quarterly Journal of Economics" for Oct., 1896, and Jan.,1897.

[2] Sumner, "History of American Currency," p. 38. In 1700, ac-

In view of such a fall in values, it is not surprising that the
people should have been unable to buy much English clothing,
and that domestic manufacture in the household should have
increased.

In the lumber districts of New Hampshire, the woolen manufacture did not thrive so well as elsewhere, but Armstrong,
the collector of customs, wrote in 1720 that within three years
about five hundred Irish families had settled in and about the
province, and had put the inhabitants on improving the linen
cloth industry for shirting and sheeting. The woolen manufacture had gone on in the other colonies, he said, and the assemblies had encouraged the coming of artists to teach the
people to manufacture their own produce. This industry had
been brought to such perfection that thousands of pounds'
worth of stuffs and druggets were sold in the Boston shops.
" Since New England is capable of producing their own manufacture in woolen, linen, iron, copper, etc.," he adds, " they are
now fully bent that nothing shall divert them from it. I presume in a few years they will set up for themselves, independent
from England." There were more than 30,000 sheep, at this
time, on some of the Massachusetts islands,[1] and the wool was
yearly transported to the several colonies to be manufactured,
in spite of the law against this practice. A letter from John
Iskyll, of the custom house in Boston, bears similar testimony.[2] The country people in New York were still making a
little homespun of flax and wool, in 1746, " to supply themselves somewhat with necessities of clothing,"[3] but they seem to
have bought from Massachusetts. In a cargo sent from Boston
to Albany, in 1756, were 200 homespun jackets.[4] A society was
formed in New York, in 1765, to encourage the home manu-

cording to Bellomont, £1000 colonial currency—£700 sterling; in
Andros's day £750 colonial currency—£600 sterling. B. T. New
Eng., H: 34, 43.
[1] Cf. p. 129.
[2] Mr. Armstrong to the Board of Trade, B. T. New Eng., X: 80.
[3] Docts. rel. to New York, Vol. VI, p. 511.
[4] Weeden, p. 679.

facture of woolens. The members pledged themselves not to
import cloth, nor to eat the meat of sheep or lambs.[1]

The interest of Massachusetts in spinning amounted to the
enthusiasm of a modern " craze." On the anniversary of the
Boston Society for Promoting Industry and Frugality, in 1749,
three hundred " young female spinsters spun at their wheels
on the Common ; " and the old town-house at Charlestown was
turned into a spinning-school that year.[2] The Court granted
£15,000 to erect a spinning-house, and it was proposed that one
person should come from each town for instruction.[3] In 1757,
a tax on carriages was assigned to the benefit of the linen
industry.[4]

From the above outline of the progress of manufactures in
the colonies, it will be seen that no very accurate estimate can
be made of the amount of woolen or other manufactures. Quo-
tations from odd sources might be multiplied, but those given
are samples of the rest. Governors' reports to the Board of
Trade cannot be wholly relied upon. One governor, in his
righteous zeal for the commercial interest for the mother-country, exaggerated the offenses of the colonists ; while another,
with a desire to represent his flock as white sheep and to pro-
pitiate the home government, minimizes the extent of the
growing industries and attributes them to the absolute necessity of the people, not to their desire to injure the trade of Great
Britain.

A few general conclusions, however, are obvious. The area
of manufacture was the north, and not the south. It is interesting to note that the only occasions on which the southern colonies entered into the manufacture of clothing, to any extent
worth mentioning, were when their natural staples, either failed
to make returns for importation,[5] or became a drug in the mar-

---

[1] Bolles, Chapter on " Manufactures."
[2] Weeden, p. 679.
[3] Mass. Archives, LIX, 361, quoted by Weeden.
[4] Mass. Archives, LIX, 347, quoted by Weeden.
[5] See the case of Maryland in Col. Hart's Report of 1720. B. T.
Plants. Gen., Entry Bk., Jan. 23, 1734.

ket.[1] There was little to induce Carolina, Maryland or Virginia to set up manufactures, for their great staples found a steady market, and their exports to Great Britain approached, and after the middle of the eighteenth century equaled, or even exceeded, their imports ; while the northern provinces fell steadily behind. South Carolina, Maryland, and especially Virginia, suffered comparatively little from the lack of coin, because they were able to trade directly with England.[2] It is probable that South Carolina, which produced more pitch and tar than all the other colonies together, would not have engaged in manufactures, even if the raising of naval stores had never been introduced, since her chief product was rice. New England and New York, where the British government had made the most strenuous efforts to stimulate the production of pitch and tar, produced very little of those commodities for export, and made more homespun clothing and manufactured articles than all the other colonies together.

It is true that the exports from New England to Great Britain never caught up with the imports, so that the jealously guarded balance of trade inclined properly toward the mother-country ; but, on the other hand, there seems to be no doubt that the attempts to kill manufactures by forcing the production of naval stores on New England, was a failure. How far that failure was due to that perversity of the people of which the surveyors of the woods complained, cannot be computed ; but if the history of the trade in naval stores teaches anything, it is, first, that the colonies understood their own interests better than the Board of Trade ; and, in the second place, that through lack of a true understanding of the economic conditions in America and by

---

[1] Macpherson notes, in his Annals of Commerce, Vol. III, p. 260, that an overstock of rice in Carolina, in 1743, when the war with France broke out, put the people upon trying to employ their negroes on sundry new manufactures of linen and woolen, which they were before accustomed to take from Great Britain, and of which "their mother-country would soon have become jealous, had not, fortunately for them, the true indigo plant happened to be discovered just then."

[2] Bruce, "Economic History of Virginia," Vol. II, p. 395.

contradictory measures the home government helped rather
than hindered the economic revolution which preceded the
political separation of the colonies from the mother-country.
In other words, England in attempting, according to the received colonial policy of the age, to exploit the plantations failed
to appreciate the fact that the colonists were working out, unconsciously for the most part, a commercial independence
which the physical conditions of the country and the natural
operation of economic laws rendered inevitable. The statesmen and economists of the seventeenth and eighteenth cen-
turies vaguely suspected the truth and groped after a way of
escape, but, not fully comprehending the case, they let the colonies alone when other matters were, for the time, more pressing,
and, again, as some warning from over the water recalled their
fears lest the mercantile system was not working itself out properly in the colonies, sought to regulate the course of trade by
restrictive legislation.

If only the men who possessed the genius, or the common
sense, to take advantage of the natural conditions of commercial activity in America and to reconcile the interests of the colonists with those of the mother-country, had controlled the
policy of England, it might have been possible to divert successfully the otherwise inevitable course of commercial autonomy.

APPENDIX A.
Price Lists of Naval Stores. (1692-1704.)

		Per	Year.	£ s. d.	£ s. d.	£ s. d.
Col. Fletcher's Prices in New York. B. T. Plants. Gen., C : 5.			1696.			
	Tar,	last,	12— 0— 0			
	Hemp,	cwt.	38— 4			
Navy Prices. B. T. Plants. Gen., C : 4.	Tar,	last,	11—12— 6			
	Hemp,	cwt.	26— 6 to 27— 6			
Prices of East Country Stores. B. T. Plants. Gen., C : 5.			Just before the war.	1692.	Since the war.	
	Tar,	last,	6— 4— 0	11—12— 6	11— 5— 0 to 12— 7— 6	
	Hemp,	cwt.	20—10	27—10	22—10 " 27—10	
	Pitch,	ton,	6— 4— 0	9—12— 6	9—12— 6 " 10—15— 0	
Prices offered at bearing. March, 1694. B. T. Plants. Gen., C : 19.		(N. Eng.)	1694.			
	Tar,	last,	2—13— 0			
Allen & Co. B. T. New Eng., C. 20.			1694			
	Tar,	last,	13— 4— 0			
	Pitch,	cwt.	20			
Evance. (Goods in England,) B. T. New Eng., C : 23.	Tar,	last,	13— 4— 0			
	Pitch,	ton,	20— 0— 0			
	Hemp,	ton,				
Slye. (Goods in Maryland.) B. T. New Eng. C : 23.	Tar,	last,	5— 4— 0			
	Pitch,	ton,	4—16— 0			
	Hemp,	ton,	14— 0— 0			

	Per	Year 1698.		
		£ s. d.	£ s. d.	
Prices given by ... ... (in New Eng.) R. T. New Eng. ?: 22.	Tar,	last,	7—14— 0	
	Rosin.	cwt.		14— 0
		1698.		
Carolina Prices quoted by ... ... R. T. New Eng., ?: 22.	Tar,	last,	4— 4— 0	
	Pitch,	cwt.	19— 0	
		1700.		
From Whiston's "Price Current," quoted by ... R. T. New Eng., Entry Book C., June ?, 1700	Stock-holm tar,	last,	11—10— 0	
	Pitch,	last,	14— 0— 0	
	Carolina Tar,	last,	9— 4— 0	
	Pitch,	last,	17—10— 0	
		1702.		
Mayhew's Prices, R. T. Plants. Gen., D: ?.	Tar,	last,	8— 0— 0	Custom free.
	Pitch,	last,	10—10— 0	
		1702.		
Penn. Co. (in Carolina.) R. T. New Eng., N: 5.	Tar,	last,	4—14— 0	
	Pitch,	cwt.	10— 0	
		1704.		
Partridge. R. T. New Eng., O: 37.	Tar,	last.	24— 0— 0	
		1704.		
Shippen & Waterhouse, N. T. Plants. Gen., G: 21.	Tar,	last,	38— 0— 0	
	Pitch,	ton,	14— 0— 3	
		1704.		
Bridger. R. T. New Eng., Entry Book ?, May 2, 1704.	Tar,	last,	12—15— 0	
	Pitch,	cwt.	1— 3— 0	
		1704.		
Virginia. Tar made from knots. R. T. New Eng., Entry Book ?, March 16, 1704.	Tar,	last,	6— 0— 0 to 7— 4— 0	
	Pitch,	Barrel,	29— 0 to 32— 0	

FROM WHENCE.	Pr. of Pln.	M.	MASTS.			TOTAL OF MASTS.		
			great.	mid.	small.	great.	mid.	small.
... rest of Europe. The Plantations.....		11				118		
... rest of Europe. The Plantations.....								
... rest of Europe. The Plantations.....						718	100	1,200
... rest of Europe. The Plantations.....				17				
... rest of Europe. The Plantations.....				1,000	2,000	1,000	1,817	2,457
... rest of Europe. The Plantations.....			1,000			1,000		1,100
... rest of Europe. The Plantations.....		1		1,370		1,716	1,607	2,400
... rest of Europe. The Plantations.....				111				
... rest of Europe. The Plantations.....					2,000	1,176		2,200
... rest of Europe. The Plantations.....	1					1,067	1,400	677
... rest of Europe. The Plantations.....	1			1,900		1,001	604	600
... rest of Europe. The Plantations.....	0					1,200	1,002	2,000
... rest of Europe. The Plantations.....	1	0	1,	1,	2,	2,002	2,100	3,007
... rest of Europe. The Plantations.....	0	14		1,	1,	600	1,004	5,000
... rest of Europe. The Plantations.....	2	9	191	1,	2,	700	1,007	2,000
... rest of Europe. The Plantations.....								
... rest of Europe. The Plantations.....								
... rest of Europe. The Plantations.....								

B. T.
Trade Papers,
pp.

BIBLIOGRAPHY.

Ashley, John. Trade and Revenue of the British Colonies in America, 1743.

"Acts and Laws of Massachusetts Bay," Edition of 1742.

Bancroft, George. History of the United States of America, Edition of 1885.

— Beer, George L. The Commercial Policy of England Toward the American Colonies, New York, 1893.

Belknap, Jeremy. History of New Hampshire, Edition of 1791.

Bishop, J. Leander. History of American Manufactures, 1878.

Board of Trade Papers, (In Public Record Office, London).
    Journals, Nos. 7-68.
    Trade Papers, Nos. 4-6, 23.
    Miscellanies, Nos. 1-9, 11-13.
    Maryland, Nos. 5-6.
    New England, Nos. 5-30, 342, 45-47.
    New Hampshire, Nos. 1-4, 8.
    New York, Nos. 4-35, 121-122.
    Plantations General, Nos. 2-16, 34-44.
    Proprieties, Nos. 2-20.
    America and West Indies, No. 1.

Bolles, A. S. Industrial History of the United States.

" Britannia Languens," 1680.

─ Brougham, Henry. Enquiry into the Colonial Policy of the European Powers, 1803.

Bruce, P. A. Economic History of Virginia in the Seventeenth Century, 1896.

Burnaby, Andrew. Travels Through the Middle Settlements in North America, 1680.

Chalmers, G. Introduction to the History of the Revolt of the American Colonies.

Child, Josiah. New Discourse on Trade, 1693. (First Edition, 1692).

Coke, Roger. Considerations on the State of the Northern Colonies.

Cunningham, William. Growth of English Industry and Commerce in Modern Times, 1892.

D'Avenant, Charles. Political and Commercial Works.

De Foe. Essay on Projects, 1697.
    A Plan of English Commerce.

Douglass, William. A Discourse Concerning the Currencies of the British Plantations in America, etc. Reprinted in American Economic Association Studies, 1897.

Doyle, J. A. The English Colonies in America, 1882.

"Essay on the Trade of the Northern Colonies of Great Britain in North America." Philadelphia Reprint of 1764.

Evelyn, John. Diary and Correspondence, Bohn Edition, 1884.

Felt. History of the Massachusetts Currency.

Force, Peter. The Force Tracts. (British Museum.)

Ford, W. C. (Editor.) Report on the Trade of Great Britain and the United States, 1791. Edition of 1888.

Fortrey, Samuel. England's Interest and Improvement.

Gee, Joshua. The Trade and Navigation of Great Britain Considered, 1731, (First Edition, 1729).

Greene, G. W. Historical View of the American Revolution, Fifth Edition.

Hakluyt. Voyages of the English Nation to America, Goldsand's Edition, 1889.

Hall, F. Importance of the British Plantations in America; the State of Their Trade, etc., 1731.

Hewins, W. A. S. English Trade and Finance in the Seventeenth Century, 1892.

— Hutchinson, Thomas. History of the Province of Massachusetts Bay from 1691-1750, 1768.

"Importance of the British Plantations," anon., 1731.

—"Interest of the Merchants and Manufacturers of Great Britain in the Present Contest with the Colonies Stated and Considered," London, 1774.

Johnson, Capt. Edward. Wonder-Working Providence of Sion's Saviour in New England.

Johnston, John. History of the Towns of Bristol and Bremen in the State of Maine, including the Settlement at Pemaquid, 1873.

Kapp, Friedrich. Die Deutsche im Staate New York während des achtzehn Jahrhunderts. New York, 1884.

Lecky, W. E. H. History of England in the Eighteenth Century.

"Letter to a Member of Parliament Concerning the Naval Stores Bill," 1720.

Macpherson, David. Annals of Commerce, Manufactures, Fisheries and Navigation, London, 1805.

Massachusetts in New England, Records of Governor and Company of, Shurtleff's Edition.

Massachusetts Historical Society Collections.

Mitchell, Dr. J. Present State of Great Britain and North America, 1767.

Morton, Thomas. The New England Canaan, 1632.

Neal, Daniel. History of New England, 1747.

New Hampshire, Documents Relating to. Called the "Province Papers," 1623-1686. 10 vols.

New York, Documents Relating to the Colonial History of. Edited by E. B. O'Callaghan. 15 vols.

O'Callaghan, E. B. Documentary History of the State of New York, 1850. 4 vols.

Palfrey, J. G. History of New England, 1858-1890. 5 vols.

Parliamentary Debates in England. London, 1761. 32 vols.

Patton, J. H. Natural Resources of the United States, 1894.

Pennsylvania Magazine of History and Biography, Vols. 1-17.

Pennsylvania, Minutes of the Provincial Council of, Philadelphia, 1852. 17 vols.

Pollexfen, Sir H. Discourse of Trade and Paper Credit, 1697.

Postlethwayt, M. Works of. Whitworth's Revision, 1771.

"Present State of Great Britain with Regard to Agriculture, Population, and Manufactures, Impartially Considered," London, 1767.

Purry, Wm. and Three Others. Description of Carolina, 1731.

Raynal, Abbé. A Philosophical and Political History of the British Settlement and Trade in North America. Transl. from the French, 1776.

Roberts, Ellis H. New York. (Commonwealth Series.)

Rogers, J. E. Thorold. Industrial and Commercial History of England, 1892.

Sainsbury, W. Noel. Calendar of State Papers. Colonial Series. America and West Indies, 1574-1680. 5 vols.

Saunders, Wm. L. The Colonial Records of North Carolina, 1886.

Scharfe and Westcott. History of Philadelphia, 1884.

Seeley, J. R. The Expansion of England, 1895.

Smith, Adam. Wealth of Nations, Roger's Edition, 1880.

"State of Importation from Great Britain Into the Port of Boston from January, 1770."

Statutes at Large, of England.

Statutes of the Realm. Records Commission Edition.

Sumner, Wm. G. History of American Currency, 1884.

Virginia, A Perfect Description of. 1649. Force Tracts, No. VIII.

Waltershausen, A. Sartorious Freiherrn von. Die Arbeitsverfassung der Englischen Kolonien in Nord Amerika, 1894.

Weeden, Wm. B. Economic and Social History of New England, (1620-1789), 1891.

Williamson. History of Maine,(1602-1820.) Hallowell Edition, 1832.

Willis, Wm. Paper on the Scotch-Irish Immigration to Maine. (In Collections of the Maine Historical Society. Vol. VI.)

INDEX.

JOHNS HOPKINS UNIVERSITY STUDIES

IN

Historical and Political Science.

Herbert B. Adams, Editor.

Other papers will be announced from time to time.

THE JOHNS HOPKINS PRESS,

BALTIMORE, MD.

Extra Volumes of Studies

— IN —

HISTORICAL AND POLITICAL SCIENCE.

The extra volumes are sold at reduced rates to regular subscribers to the Studies.

The set of fifteen (regular) series is now offered, uniformly bound in cloth, for library use, for $45, and including subscription to the current (sixteenth) series, for $48.

The fifteen series, with fifteen extra volumes, altogether thirty volumes, in cloth as above, for $65.

All business communications should be addressed to

THE JOHNS HOPKINS PRESS, Baltimore, Maryland.